FORCES

OF THE WILD

FORCES

OF THE WILD

VICTORIA COULES

BLANDFORD

For Michael

with gratitude, and probably with love

ACKNOWLEDGEMENTS

There are many people without whom this book could never have been created, and I would like to thank them all for their help and encouragement.

At Partridge Films, Michael Rosenberg suggested the idea for the television series three years ago, and encouraged Steve Nicholls and his team to take the series in the direction it wanted to go. His creative input, advice and guidance was always appreciated, and, together with Mark Broughton and Jayne Clarke, he provided the practical support from Partridge Films that allowed the series to come alive.

This book cannot exist in isolation from the series, and as scriptwriter on the series, and, later, author of this book, I extend my grateful thanks to the people at Partridge Films who gave me such invaluable help.

Mark Hammond took on the daunting task of organizing the many photographic illustrations for the book as well as providing background research for the book and scripts. Victoria Webb also assisted me with research for the scripts; they were both a crucial part of the writing process. The computer animations were produced by Steve Root at Science Pictures Ltd, and many members of the team provided their photographs for the book. Keith Ribbons created the superb additional illustrations.

The rest of the *Forces of the Wild* team made the experience of working on the series a great pleasure: Grant McDowell, Clare Dornan, Katherine Seward, Daniela Pulverer, Ann Parker, Liz O'Brien, Sarah Sapper, Sophie Mead, and Jacqueline Marheineke. The many cameramen brought back stunning images, and the editors Martin Elsbury, Tim Coope, Peter Brownlee, Stuart Napier, Graham Shrimpton and Vincent Pipe worked long and hard to create the programmes. Gina Fucci and her team at Films@59 took care of the post-production process, and Mark Knights of TK Films transferred uncountable hours of film to videotape. Ian Butcher and Steven Faux composed, and occasionally performed, the beautiful music that added a whole new dimension to the series. I thank Oliver Ledbury for his invaluable help with proofreading the text.

I am grateful to Charles Walker at Peters, Fraser and Dunlop for putting faith in me as a writer. At Cassell, Stuart Booth kept faith with the idea of this book from the very beginning; Antonia Maxwell, Alison Copland and Rosie Anderson gently guided me through the process of editing, and the design team at Cassell put everything behind the creation of the book.

If I have omitted anyone, it is not my intention to do so, as so many people were a part of *Forces of the Wild*. Yet, last, I thank my husband, friend and partner, Steve Nicholls, for supporting me, encouraging me, reading the text and making suggestions that reflected my thoughts and ideas. I thank him for his faith in me, and for always being there.

A Blandford Book
First published in the UK 1999 by Blandford
a Cassell imprint

Cassell plc
Wellington House
125 Strand
London WC2R 0BB

Text © Victoria Coules 1999

Distributed in the United States by
Sterling Publishing Co., Inc.
387 Park Avenue South
New York, NY 10016-8810

A Cataloguing-in-Publication Data entry for this title is available from the British Library

ISBN 0-7137-2745-4

Designed by Grahame Dudley Associates
Printed and bound in Great Britain by Bath Press, Bath

Contents

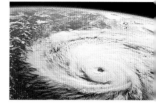

Introduction

In August 1992, while filming on the east coast of Florida, we were staying at a beach hotel near Fort Pierce. We would get up early to film the tiny white ghost crabs that came onto the beach at dawn and were the subject of a wildlife film. During the day we were working alongside the scientists at a Smithsonian Institution laboratory at Fort Pierce. But, suddenly, we were rudely interrupted by an unwelcome guest.

Hurricane Andrew was making its relentless way towards the Florida coast, and on the night of Saturday 22 August, the Hurricane Watch for the east coast was upgraded to a Hurricane Warning. By the Sunday morning, at breakfast, we were told that the hotel was closing and we had to leave. The order had gone out to evacuate the area and so, along with hundreds of thousands of others in south Florida, we packed up and drove north and inland, to Orlando where the Disneyworld complex had spawned hundreds of motels.

Hurricane Andrew roared into the coast just south of Miami, at 3 am on Monday 24 August. When we woke up in our hotel room in Orlando, we switched on the television news; at first there was nothing, as if the whole event had been a dreadful nightmare. Then an announcer said that they knew Hurricane Andrew had made landfall, but no one could get any news reports out of the area. Gradually, during the course of the morning, the news of the terrible devastation reached the media, and the whole world witnessed the results of Andrew's wrath.

Hurricane Andrew was a shock because the storm had had the affront to attack the most powerful nation on the globe. Yet hurricanes are a natural force of nature, a part of the interplay between the atmosphere and the ocean, the motion of the air across the Earth that can be the subtle touch of a breeze or the destructive roar of a hurricane or tornado.

Over the thousands of years of civilization we have become detached from the natural cycles of the planet. Cocooned in our cities, we live by artificial time. How many of you reading this know the phase of the moon today, or which constellations will appear in the night sky? Everything we need to live comes from the Earth, and, over time, we have turned our backs on her.

Many programmes appear on popular television that treat volcanoes, earthquakes, storms and floods as disasters, and we watch in morbid fascination the destruction they bring. They are a never-ending source of stories for the film industry, or for theme parks where we can experience the thrill of an earthquake or a volcano in safety. Yet, as one Japanese writer pointed out, it is not the earthquake that kills people, it is their possessions. But, even though these upheavals of the planet are destructive, they are as much a part of our living on the Earth as the sunshine and rain. More than that, they serve to give us a sense of perspective of our place in this world.

Forces of the Wild – the television series and this book – is the story of the Earth. It tells of the ongoing processes

Planet Earth – our home planet

that make it a dynamic, living planet, of life and of the relationships between humans and the world that sustain us. There are many different views of the world, from the Judaeo-Christian philosophy that the Earth is there to support the human race through to the animist beliefs of many tribal cultures. Yet the Earth itself continues on its own way, despite us. If humans disappeared off the face of the planet tomorrow, it would still sweep around the sun, its tides responding to the pull of the moon. The Earth's hot interior would still churn, the continents would still move across the globe, and life – nature – would adapt and change,

evolution and extinction being part of the same process.

The television series was constrained to less than five hours, and so many of the ideas and stories were limited by time and the medium. This book expands many of these ideas and explores territory that the series did not include. It goes beyond the series, to show how many of the Earth's processes work, how they affect us, and how life itself is one of the forces that shape and change the planet.

PART ONE
ICE AND FIRE

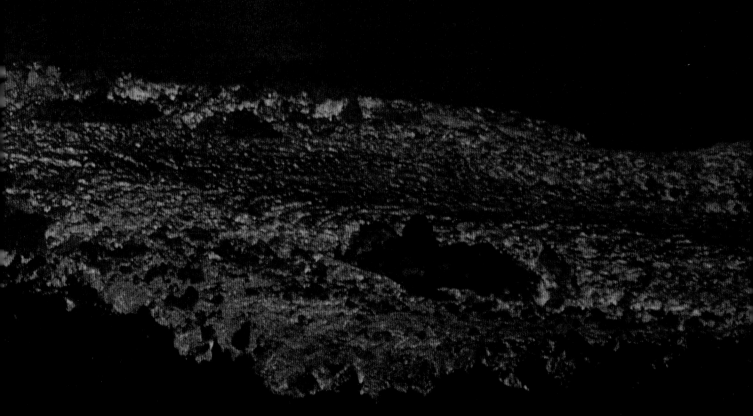

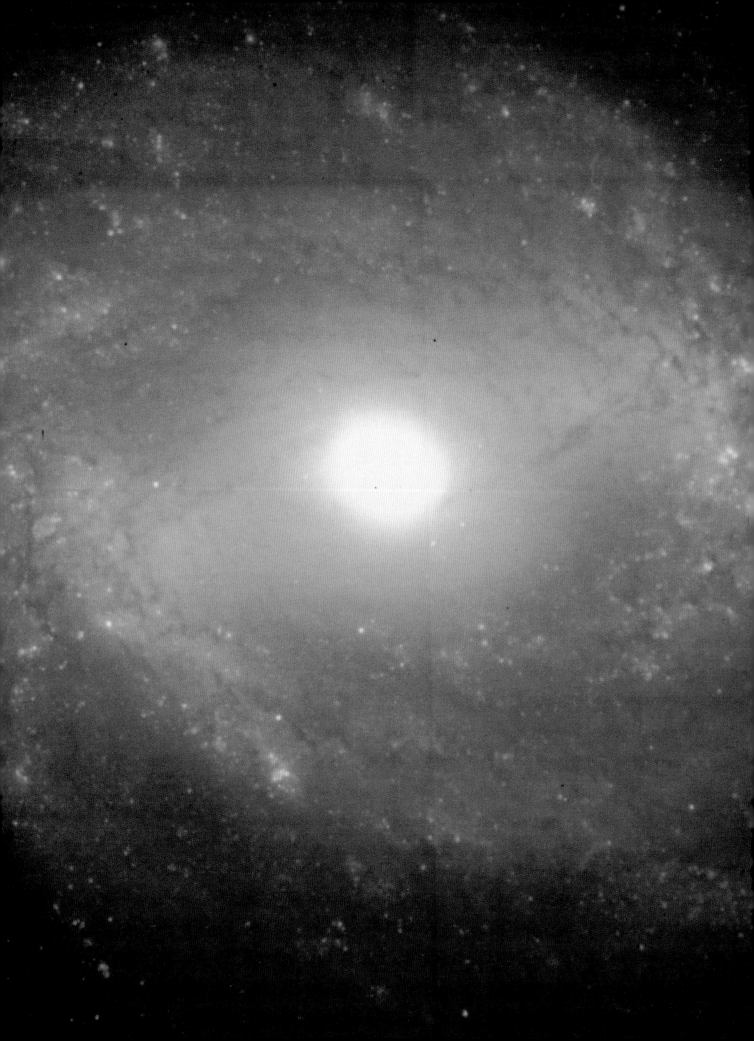

chapter 1

A Star is Born

It was at the beginning, when nothing was; sand was not,

nor sea, nor cool waves.

Earth did not exist, nor heaven on high.

The mighty gap was, but no growth.

Edda – *ancient Icelandic saga*

Beginnings are always difficult, and none more so than this. Where do we start? Our ancestors must have looked around them and, once they had found food and shelter, they must have wondered about the light and dark, the sun and moon, the seasons, the passing of time. And as they wondered they must have made connections, developed language, and asked questions.

It is hard for us to understand, now, what they must have felt as they faced death, or watched the stars wheel overhead, or heard the voice of the thunder. But their questions would not have been so different from the ones we ask today.

Where do we come from? Where did the world come from? The finest minds throughout the history of humanity have addressed these questions; almost every culture on Earth has its own version of the answer.

The Judaeo-Christian story tells us how God created the Heaven and Earth; how the Earth was without form, how darkness was upon the face of the deep. How God said,

Light from this distant galaxy has taken 78 million years to reach us

'Let there be light', and there was light. To the ancient Egyptians, the sun-god Ra emerged from Nun, the Primordial Waters of Chaos, of nothing. Ra has two other names: Atum, meaning 'he who completes, or perfects' and Kephri, meaning 'he who comes into being'. And Ra-Atum-Kephri created the first pair of gods, Shu ('air') and Tefnut ('moisture'), who in turn created Geb, the Earth, and Nut, the Sky. The ancient Icelandic sagas tell that before any worlds were formed there was nothing – just darkness and silence, an empty void, *Ginnungagap*.

Quaint stories, it seems. But when we consider the explanation offered by science, maybe their stories are not so quaint. Maybe they are just a different way of looking at the world.

So. To begin at the beginning.

We live on the Earth, a relatively small planet, one of nine planets orbiting the sun. And the sun? It is an average sort of star, travelling through space, the planets travelling with it. Looking at the night sky, there are stars as far as the eye can see, and beyond, so what is different about the sun? Nothing.

The sun is one of many stars, one of billions of stars

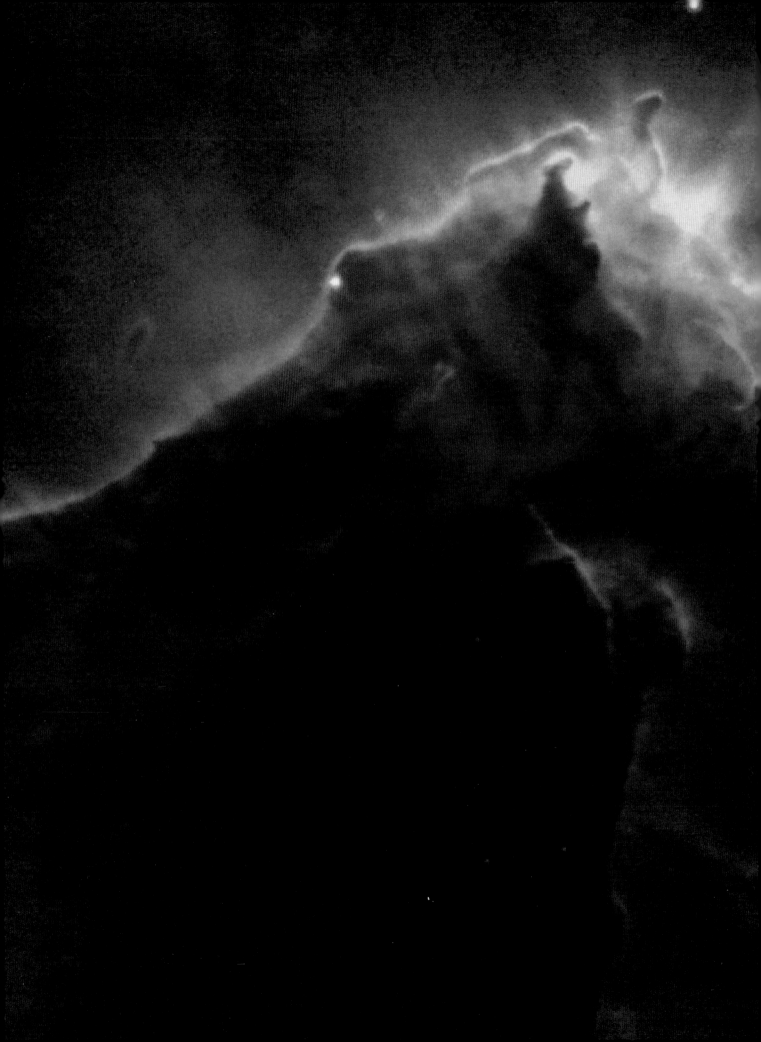

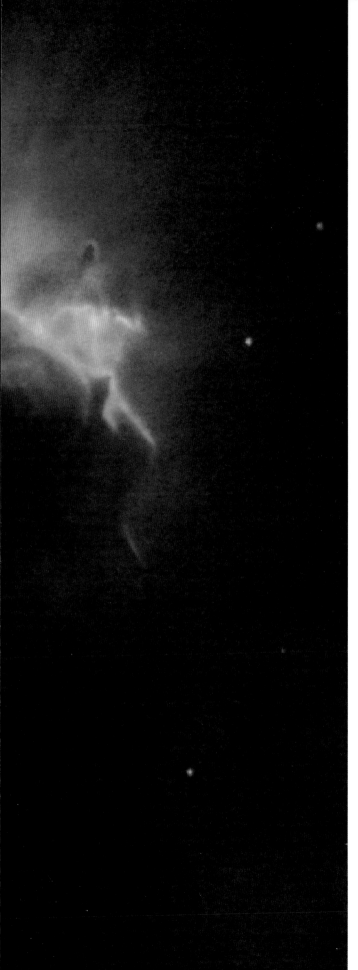

grouped in a galaxy, which looks rather like a cosmic disc-shaped pin-Catherine wheel in space, and the Earth is about two-thirds from the centre of this galaxy. On a clear night, the dark background of the sky has a filmy, misty stripe running across it: the Milky Way. This is our galaxy, an edge-on view, a swathe of stars so distant that we get only a hint of their light.

The problem with thinking about galaxies is the vast distances involved. To get some idea, we can consider the speed of light. To our eyes and brains, it seems instantaneous; we look at something and we see what we are looking at.

But light has a fixed speed. It travels at 300,000 km (186,000 miles) a second; not a lot of help until we realize it takes about eight minutes for the light of the sun to reach us. But if the sun is a star, how far away are the other stars? Our nearest neighbour after the sun is a star called Alpha Centauri, and light from Alpha Centauri takes four years to reach us. We look at the sun, we see what it looked like eight minutes ago; we look at Alpha Centauri and see what it looked like four years ago. To find a way of describing these immense distances, we need another measurement. Astronomers use a unit of a *light* year, which is the distance that light travels in one year. It sounds like a light-year should be a description of time, but it is a very useful way of describing the vast distances of space. There is no reason why the 'light month' cannot be used as the distance it takes for light to travel in a month, or the 'light hour', or the 'light minute', but the light year is the most useful. If we look at the rest of the galaxy, the stars are so far away that their light has been travelling for tens, hundreds or thousands of years to reach us.

But it goes on.

There are billions of galaxies in the Universe, more than can be counted. They come in different shapes and sizes, but many of them are the spiral, pin-wheel shape of our own galaxy. They are all moving, and – which seems to go against common sense – they are all moving *away* from each other. The Universe is expanding, everything is flying apart and, other than that, we do not know much more.

Galaxies and an expanding Universe are a far cry from what we see when we look out of our front door; and what our ancestors would have seen when they looked out of their cave. So, to come back to the Earth, and ask where it comes from, brings us to a time about six billion years ago.

A 'star nursery', where clouds of dust and gas are condensing into nuclei that explode to become stars

Compared to the age of the Universe, this was quite recent; stars had been and gone, galaxies appeared and disappeared all before our sun even existed.

But then, somewhere in our part of the galaxy, an old star was reaching the end of its life, and, as stars do as they die, it collapsed in on itself, exploded and scattered debris across the realms of space. Some of this debris formed a cloud of dust and gas, a huge flat disc of particles, just floating in space, drifting in the darkness and emptiness. Things would have stayed much the same, except that there is a force – possibly the most fundamental force of nature – that affects everything and everybody. Gravity.

Gravity, in its basic form, means simply that everything is attracted to everything else. There are no exceptions. When Isaac Newton watched his apple fall to the ground, he realized that the apple was attracted to the Earth, *and* the Earth was attracted to the apple. But the Earth, being so much bigger, has more resistance to movement – inertia – than the apple, so the apple did most of the moving, and fell towards the Earth. The Earth *did* fall towards the apple, but its movement was so small as to be unnoticeable. If two things are the same size, they will be attracted by the same amount; if one is bigger than the other, has more 'stuff', more mass, then the smaller object moves more than the bigger object. And the closer together the two objects, the stronger the force pulling them together.

Now back to the dust cloud. Over a long period of time, under the influence of gravity, the particles in the dust cloud were attracted to each other and, gradually, the cloud started to condense at the centre. The more particles that were drawn together, the stronger the force of gravity, so more and more particles were drawn to the centre. The cloud was beginning to collapse in on itself.

Time passed.

At the centre of the cloud, the particles were getting closer and closer together, and, the closer they got, the stronger the pull of gravity was between them. The cloud was condensing at the centre, and, as the particles of dust and gas became more and more tightly packed, they grew hotter and hotter. There was so much material in the cloud that this process became a vicious circle; the bigger – and more dense – the nucleus of the cloud became, the stronger the effect of gravity; the stronger the effect of gravity, the more stuff was drawn into the nucleus.

Far away galaxies revealed by the Hubble telescope – their light has taken billions of years to reach Earth

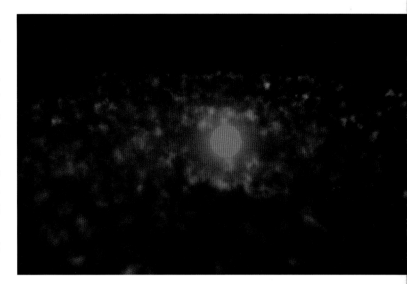

Particles in the dust cloud are drawn to the centre

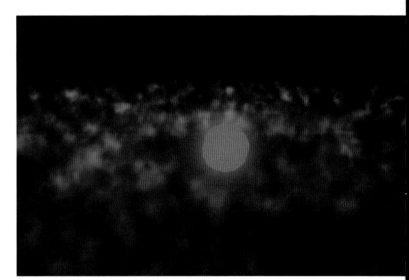

A nucleus forms at the centre of the cloud

Pressure and heat trigger a massive nuclear explosion

A STAR IS BORN

Eventually, something had to give. A limit had been reached; the combination of heat and pressure became so intense that it triggered a massive nuclear chain reaction. In a huge explosion, heat – and light – flashed through the cloud, and created a massive ball of burning gas. This was a new star – our sun.

When the sun was ignited, over 99 per cent of the dust cloud was captured in this cosmic inferno. But the sun does not burn in the same way as fire on Earth; the sun is a massive nuclear reactor. Whereas the atom bomb gets its energy from splitting the atom, the sun is continually fusing atoms – hydrogen, the simplest element, is under such high temperature and pressure that the atoms are forced together, and combine to create a new element, helium.

This is *nuclear fusion*, which generates vast amounts of energy. The process is not infinite – eventually the sun will run out of material – but it has been burning for billions of years and will do so for several billion years yet. When it first came to life, the sun was bigger and cooler than it is now; as it burns, it contracts and gets hotter, all part of the natural life cycle of a star. Today, the sun is roughly 30 per cent hotter than it was when it was born.

Meanwhile, the other 1 per cent of the dust cloud was circling round the sun, still in the flat disc shape, all moving round in an anticlockwise direction. Tiny grains of dust and

The surface of the sun, our own star, is in constant turmoil as energy is released in the form of heat and light

The Burning Sun

The sun is our own, personal star, the centre of the solar system. Compared to the Earth, it is massive; approximately 109 times the diameter of the Earth, at a huge 1,392,000 km (865,000 miles). It has more than 300,000 times more mass than the Earth, and is 150 million km (93 million miles) away.

The sun contains more than 99 per cent of the matter in the solar system, but it is made up mainly from the light gases hydrogen and helium, with only 2 per cent of any other elements present. And it is a continual nuclear fusion reactor.

Being so big, the sun's gravity compresses all its material towards its centre, where the heat and the pressure is extremely high. Hydrogen, the simplest of the atoms, normally consists of a nucleus, which is just one particle, called a *proton*, and a much smaller particle, an *electron*, in orbit round the nucleus. Inside the sun, the heat and pressure strip off the electrons, and force the protons so close together that they combine to form a new element, helium, whose nucleus consists of two protons and two other particles, *neutrons*.

This process also releases energy in the

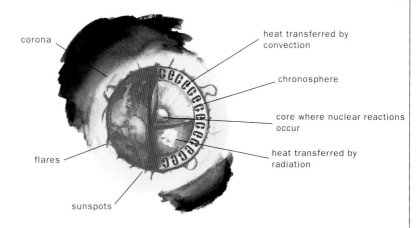

The structure of the sun

corona
heat transferred by convection
chronosphere
core where nuclear reactions occur
heat transferred by radiation
flares
sunspots

form of gamma rays, a high-energy form of X-ray. But all this is happening deep inside the sun; the energy takes about 1,000 years to get to the surface where it is released as heat and light. The process of creating a new element from a simpler one is called *nuclear fusion*, and will continue until it has turned all the hydrogen into helium. The sun is about halfway through this process, so will keep going for another four or five billion years.

Like everything else in the solar system, the sun is rotating, but, because it is made of gas, it does not all rotate at the same speed. The gases round the equator take 25 days,

whereas those at the poles take nearer 36 days. This violent, fast rotation of burning gases creates a strong magnetic field that is continually changing, causing the gases themselves to churn and bubble up from the surface.

Sometimes the magnetic field distorts, creating patches on the sun's surface that are slightly cooler than the surrounding gas, so they look darker. These are sunspots, and seem to come in cycles of 11 years; it is thought that when there are many sunspots they affect the climate of the Earth, although how they do has yet to be explained.

ice began to fuse together, forming bigger lumps, and as the bigger lumps swept round in their orbits they collided with each other. Gradually, these lumps grew bigger, until they formed substantial-sized rocky lumps, the *planetesimals*. Each was orbiting on its own path, forming concentric rings around the sun. Any other rocks that were in the way would collide with the planetesimal and combine with it, adding to its bulk. This process, of lumps colliding and combining, is called accretion. And *accretion* would eventually create the planets themselves.

The emerging, embryo solar system was a place of extreme conditions.

On the one hand, close to the sun, the heat and radiation was so intense that most materials were burnt off into space. Small, solid planets formed, the most hot and dense being Mercury. It is made of heavy materials like iron, and has no atmosphere; any light materials are just burnt away.

On the other hand, much further out from the sun, the

planets were very different. The sun's warmth has little effect here, and the sun appears as a bright distant star. It is so cold that everything freezes. Even light gases like hydrogen and helium condense, captured by gravity in the same way that the dust cloud was concentrated. This is the realm of the huge planets known as the *gas giants*. Jupiter, Saturn, Uranus and Neptune, are huge; Jupiter is so big – over 300 times the mass of the Earth – that it almost reached the point where it, too, collapsed and exploded; it almost became a star in its own right. Happily for us, it stayed as a planet, although a rather strange one by our standards; Jupiter has an atmosphere, but no solid surface. An indestructible spaceship approaching the planet would descend through dense clouds of hydrogen, helium and methane, which become liquid, until at the very centre is *solid* hydrogen under unimaginable pressure. In the turmoil of the atmosphere is Jupiter's most famous feature – its 'great red spot', a roaring hurricane, twice the diameter of the Earth.

Jupiter, the great 'gas giant', is the largest object in the solar system after the sun itself

Its neighbour, Saturn, is similar in structure, but is more famous for its rings. They are not solid, but consist of fragments of rock and ice particles that make them glitter. Although Saturn is almost as big as Jupiter, the rings are only a kilometre (just over half a mile) thick, with complex patterns of at least 10,000 different bands.

Uranus and Neptune are similar gas giants, although Uranus travels round the sun on its side, rolling over and over rather than spinning like a top as do the rest of the planets. And, at the very edge of the solar system, small, dark, solid Pluto makes its way round the sun on an orbit more eccentric than that of the other planets.

Between the orbits of Mars and Jupiter, some of the lumps in the solar system were never destined to build planets. They formed the asteroids, a motley collection of fragments of rock and ice, some several kilometres across, some a matter of a few metres, travelling around the sun in their own orbits.

Sometimes the solar system has visitors. Comets, some as old as the solar system itself, pass close enough to the sun to be drawn in by its gravity, and sweep round past the planets, sometimes close enough to be seen in the night sky. The glorious Hale-Bopp comet, which came so close in

The Solar System

To get some idea of the scale of the solar system, imagine the Earth the size of a golfball. The moon would be a ball with a diameter the size of a penny, orbiting the Earth at a distance of 12 cm (5 in) away.

The sun would be a burning ball of gas, 4.5 m (15ft) high – more than twice the height of a man – at a distance of 500 m (1,650 ft). The arrangement of the planets in the solar system is in the shape of a disc, so the other planets would also be on the same plane. Mercury would be a third of the size of the Earth, about the size of a hazelnut, 180 m (600 ft) out from the sun. And Venus, roughly the same size as the Earth, is 340 m out from the sun.

Further out from the Earth, the planet Mars is about half the size of the Earth, a distance of 700 m (2,300 ft) from the sun.

The huge gas giants are a long way from the sun. Jupiter would be a ball nearly 50 cm (20 in) across, at a distance of 2.5 km (1½ miles) from the sun. And Saturn is almost the same size, 40 cm (16 in) across, but orbits the sun at a distance of 4.5 km (2¾ miles). Uranus is slightly smaller at 17 cm (7 in) across, but at a distance of nearly 9 km (5½ miles) away. More or less the same size as Uranus, Neptune is 14 km (8¾ miles) away, and the tiny, mysterious Pluto, smaller than our own moon, is more than 18 km (11¼ miles) away from the model sun.

Moving from the planets that are close to the sun to the outer planets, there seems to

On the same scale of the diameters of the planets, the distances from the sun would be 100,000 times greater than shown

Earth   Jupiter

Uranus

Pluto

Mercury

Mars

Venus

Neptune

Saturn

Relative sizes and proportional distance of planets from the sun

be a pattern in their distances from the sun. Although it is not obvious for the inner planets, each of the outer planets is – approximately – twice as far from the sun as the previous one. The pattern is not precise because the orbits of the planets are not exactly circular, and these distances are their average distances from the sun.

Until the eighteenth century, Saturn was the furthest planet that could be seen with the naked eye. Working on the number patterns the astronomer Johann Boyle worked out there was a gap between Mars and Jupiter where a planet should be and there could also be other planets, beyond

the orbit of Saturn, that would also fit the pattern.

In 1781, William Herschel used a telescope to look for the next planet beyond Saturn, and eventually discovered Uranus. But astronomers searched for the 'missing' planet between Mars and Jupiter in vain until, in 1801, a small planet was found at the correct distance; this was the first of the asteroids, a collection of thousands of chunks of rock, ranging from metres to kilometres across. On our model, they would be specks of gravel, sand and dust, orbiting the sun in bands between Mars and Jupiter, just over a kilometre (half a mile) away from it.

1997, is on an orbit that brings it close to the sun every few thousand years, and the famous Halley's comet visits every 76 years. Comets are also made of rocks and ice, and have a long tail that streams out into space. The tail does not follow the direction of motion as we would intuitively expect, but is flared out like a streamer, in the direction away from the sun, in the solar wind, the rain of particles shot out by the sun as it burns.

Some comets end their lives in our solar system; the comet Shoemaker-Levy Nine came too close to Jupiter in 1994 and was captured by the huge planet. It was destroyed as it exploded on contact with Jupiter's atmosphere, an event which was followed closely by observers here on

Earth. Jupiter still bears the scars of this spectacular collision.

But in this place of extremes, of heat and cold, of light and dark, one planet was created, which, like Goldilock's porridge, is 'just right'. Of all the small, solid, planets near the sun, Mercury is much too hot, and Venus has an atmosphere which acts like a greenhouse, capturing the sun's heat, but is still too hot. Small, red Mars has a thin atmosphere that does not blanket it from the cold or radiation of space, and is a bit too far from the sun.

Between the orbits of Venus and Mars, this planet had an inauspicious beginning, but would eventually be transformed into a planet that would be unique in the solar system – even the galaxy. Planet Earth.

Brave New World

And God said 'Let the waters under the heavens be gathered together in one place and let the dry land appear'. And it was so. God called the dry land Earth and the waters that were gathered together, he called the Seas.

Genesis i. 3

The new, raw Planet Earth was a desolate, lifeless place. There was no atmosphere, no life, nothing. It had no protection from the radiation of space, and it was bombarded by meteors. The process of accretion did not happen overnight and then simply stop; there was still a lot of debris flying around as the solar system was forming, creating the nine separate planets. Some meteors were tiny specks of dust, some were huge, several kilometres across. It still happens today, even though the dust has settled, although to nothing like the extent it happened then. But at the beginning of the Earth's story the battering and bombardment it took from the meteors had a significant effect on the young planet. It began to heat up.

To understand how this happened, if we hit a nail with a hammer enough times eventually the nail (and, to a lesser degree, the hammer) will become warm. So the meteors that were hitting the Earth brought energy, which was converted to heat on impact. The heat built up, particularly in the interior where it could not escape.

Planet Earth – the blue planet

But this was not – and is not – the only source of heat for the Earth's interior. Among the materials that went into making up the Earth were certain kinds of rocks, like granite. These rocks have a special property – they are *radioactive.*

Everything in the Universe is made up of atoms, the fundamental building blocks that combine together in different proportions to create everything else. Most atoms are stable and unchanging; hydrogen stays as hydrogen, gold stays as gold, lead stays as lead, and so on. But a few elements are naturally radioactive – they consist of atoms that are unstable, in the process of decaying, changing to a stable form. Potassium-40 is in the process of changing into argon-40, uranium-235 is changing into lead-207. But as the atoms decay they emit radiation, in a form similar to X-rays, and a small amount of heat. Rocks containing these materials are also radioactive, decaying over thousands of years.

The overall heating of the Earth was slow. The radioactive decay was gradual, and the heat built up over millions of years. To get some idea of how slow this was,

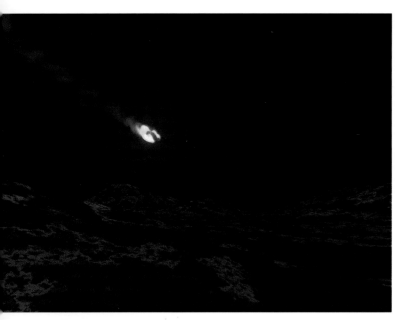

Meteors rained down onto the Earth's surface

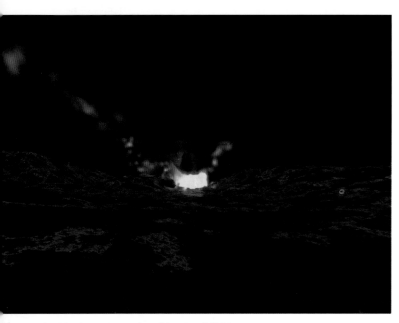

The impacts produced heat and light

we can think about how much heat a cubic centimetre of, say, granite would emit. They say a watched kettle never boils, and to boil a kettle with a cubic centimetre of granite (assuming none of the heat escaped), would take over four million years. And inside the Earth the heat could not escape, so, even though the build-up was very slow, eventually the combination of meteor collisions and radioactivity produced enough heat to melt the very rocks themselves.

It may even be that the whole planet melted. The molten rocks could flow, so the lighter elements could float while the heavier elements, like iron and nickel, sank; the

Earth was reorganizing itself into different layers, something like an onion. On the surface heat escaped into space, so it cooled, like the skin on gravy, eventually hardening, forming a solid crust. A multitude of different chemicals crystallized to form different minerals which combined together to make rocks. This thin, solid crust covers the planet, extending only tens of kilometres below the surface.

Inside the Earth, the rock was still molten, and one of the heavier elements that sank was iron. At the very centre of the planet, which was about 2,500 km (1,500 miles) in diameter, the intense pressure created a solid core of iron and nickel. But around that core, forming a layer about 2,200 km (1,400 miles) thick, the iron and nickel stayed molten, and began to flow in slow, circulating currents. This was to have a very significant effect on the Earth – it turned the whole planet into a huge magnet.

Magnetism has been known for centuries; it was a phenomenon that must have seemed like magic. Certain materials were known to attract or repel similar materials as if by an invisible force. And, allowed to swing freely, some metallic pointers always point in a certain direction – north. Magnetism *is* an invisible force, that attracts or repels in certain directions; these directions can be imagined as lines of force, shaped by the magnetic field. Different magnets have different-shaped fields; the classic way to view this is to pour iron filings on a sheet of glass and then put a magnet under the glass. The filings will align themselves in the directions of the lines of force, forming a pattern that shows the shape of the field.

However, the Earth is not a solid magnet, like a bar magnet. Its magnetism comes from the circulating currents of molten iron deep in its interior. But this iron is not magnetic, because when a metal like iron gets hot it loses its magnetic properties. To see where the Earth's magnetic field comes from, we need a short digression.

Molten iron is a very, very good conductor of electricity. And when a good conductor of electricity, like a metal wire, moves through a magnetic field, an electric current is created in the conductor. But, if an electric current *moves*, it also creates a magnetic field of its own. So the conductor moves through the magnetic field and generates an electric current, but as the conductor – and the current it generates – is still moving it creates a magnetic field, which generates an electric current, which is moving – and so on, and so on. This whole process is self-sustaining, as long as everything keeps moving; it is called a *self-exciting dynamo*. So how is this relevant to the Earth?

There are weak magnetic fields all over the solar system; one of the strongest is that of the sun. The molten layer of iron began to circulate, partly due to the rotation of the Earth. But this iron is a good conductor of electricity and it is moving through a magnetic field, so it creates a self-exciting dynamo. The moving layer, deep in the Earth's interior, turns the energy of the planet's movement into electrical and magnetic energy.

So the Earth *behaves* like a bar magnet; it has a north pole and a south pole. In the same way that a magnet can attract iron filings or pick up steel nails, so the Earth attracts any bit of magnetic material. This is the basis of the compass; like the iron filings on the glass, a freely swinging magnetic needle lines itself up along a line of force that runs north–south, between the poles. When a compass tells us which direction is north, it gives us a clue as to which direction we are going. We have used this methods for thousands of years; the Chinese knew about compasses since well before 600 BC.

There are two slight drawbacks to this system, however. The first problem is that the magnetic north pole and the true north pole are not necessarily in the same place. The true, or geographic, north and south poles are defined by the Earth's rotation; if a long stick was placed as an axis through the Earth as it spins like a top, the stick would protrude at the north and south poles. For most purposes in the last few centuries, the magnetic north pole and true north pole have been near enough to be usable for navigation, but there is a deviation that is marked on accurate charts, and the nearer we travel to the north or south pole the more the deviation. The magnetic north pole today is in the Canadian Northwest Territories, about 1,300 km (800 miles) northwest of Hudson Bay, and the south pole is on the edge of the continent of Antarctica, in Adiele Land.

The second drawback is that the different rocks that

Barnacle geese fly thousands of kilometres every year, navigating by the sun and the variations in the Earth's magnetic field

make up the Earth's crust affect the magnetic field. They create slight variations in the strength and direction of the lines of force, so inaccuracies can creep in. This effect is stronger in some places than others, so using a magnetic compass to find north does not guarantee absolute precision in direction-finding. These minor problems aside, a magnetic compass is a simple, elegant and cheap way of finding a direction, and even the most elaborate navigation systems used in aircraft or shipping still have a magnetic compass as a back-up to all the advanced inertial guidance systems and the satellite positioning systems.

We are not the only travellers to use the Earth's magnetic field for navigation, and we are certainly not the most sophisticated. Every year, barnacle geese fly for over 2,500 km (1,500 miles) from their summer nesting grounds in Greenland to a small island off the Scottish coast, Islay, to spend the

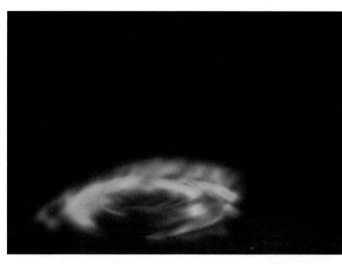

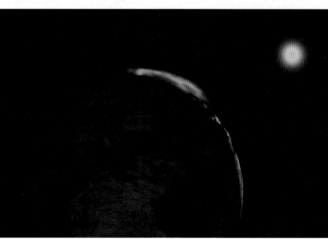

Aurora Borealis – the light show in the atmosphere dances over the North Pole

winter. When they can, they navigate by the sun, but in bad weather they also rely on the Earth's magnetic field. But they do not have a compass to tell them which is north; instead, it is thought that they sense the weak variations in the magnetic field and use them to make a mental picture of where they are – a map to guide their journey. Other creatures – whales, salmon, pigeons, even bees – use the Earth's magnetic field in the same way, navigating with astonishing accuracy.

But the Earth's magnetic field does more than guide our journeys. It helps to protect the life on the planet from the solar wind. The *solar wind* is not wind as we know it, but a stream of charged particles that are ejected from the sun as it burns, streaking towards the Earth at the speed of light. They are a form of radiation which would be deadly to us.

But as they reach the Earth most of them are trapped by the magnetic field into two layers high above the atmosphere, the Van Allen belts. Out of harm's way, most of the solar wind does not reach us, but a small fraction of these particles are deflected by the magnetic field and enter the atmosphere at the north and south poles. When they do, each particle collides with a molecule of the atmosphere. Each collision creates a flash, and a continuous stream of these collisions creates the magical, spectacular light shows, the northern and southern lights. The lights were named after the goddess of the dawn, Aurora; the northern lights are the Aurora Borealis, and the southern lights are the Aurora Australis.

Different molecules in the atmosphere flash with different colours; nitrogen flashes blue, oxygen flashes yellow and green, and the colours and displays vary with height. To the people round the Arctic, these lights took on special meanings. The Inuit around Hudson Bay, Canada, explained the northern lights:

The sky is a huge dome of hard material arched over the flat earth. On the outside there is light. In the dome there are a large number of small holes and through these holes you can see the light from the outside when it is dark. And through these holes the spirits of the dead can pass into the heavenly regions. The way to heaven leads over a narrow bridge which spans an enormous abyss. The spirits that were already in heaven light torches to guide the feet of the new arrivals. These torches are called the northern lights.

Volcanoes belched out gases, creating the Earth's first atmosphere

Ancient Continents

If we were able to go back in time and look at the Earth from space as it was 250 million years ago, it would have an ocean, and clouds, and land, but the land would bear no resemblance to a map of the Earth today.

All the land would be bunched together in a huge 'supercontinent', which geologists named *Pangaea*. This was first proposed by a German geologist, Alfred Lothar Wegener, who was one of the first to realize that the continents did indeed drift around the globe, and that there was a time when all the continents were joined as one landmass. He and his colleagues put forward their theory in 1908–1912, but it was not until the 1960s that it was finally taken seriously, as scientists found other data that confirmed the idea, and explained how it worked.

Pangaea had formed by earlier landmasses drifting towards each other, so that by 250 million years ago they had formed one continent. The original formation of the continents is not fully understood, but some of the rocks of the continents are almost as old as the Earth itself. Sea floor is continually created and destroyed, at spreading ridges and deep sea trenches, but the continents stay on top of the Earth's crust, drifting round the globe.

However, about 200 million years ago, Pangaea began to break up, with two components pulling apart in a north–south direction, forming two new continents, *Laurasia* and *Gondwanaland*. A new sea flowed along the equator, between them, the *Tethys Sea*. At the same time that Laurasia

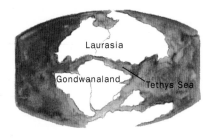

Approximately 200 million years ago

was moving away from Gondwanaland, an east–west split was beginning. South America and Africa were joined together, both a part of Gondwanaland, but they started to pull away, separating as they did so. India broke away from the remainder of Gondwanaland, and began to move north towards Laurasia, and the plate that contained Africa also moved towards Laurasia, closing the Tethys Sea.

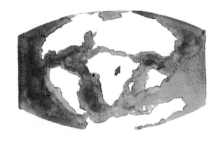

Approximately 100 million years ago

By 65 million years ago, South America had split off from Africa, and the south Atlantic Ocean was forming. Australia was beginning to separate from the remaining Gondwanaland, leaving Antarctica behind, and North America started to pull away from Europe.

Then, between 60 and 40 million years

ago, India bumped into Laurasia, creating the crumple zone that would become the Himalayas, and a plateau that would be Tibet. The Tethys Sea was closed off, forming an inland sea, the Mediterranean.

It remained for Antarctica to drift across the south pole, and the North Atlantic Ocean to open up, for the continents to be almost recognizable as they are today.

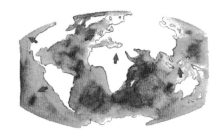

Approximately 50 million years ago

However, the process is still happening; the eastern part of Africa will split off along the Great Rift Valley, and northern Africa will close the Mediterranean Sea. Australia will continue to move north, and the Americas are still pulling away from Europe and Africa, closing the Pacific Ocean as, at the same time, the Atlantic Ocean widens.

Movement 50 million years into the future

But let us return to the newly forming, cooling Earth, four billion years ago. Between the core and the surface a rocky, more or less solid, layer formed, the *mantle* – 'more or less' because a thin layer of the mantle under the Earth's crust, the *asthenosphere*, is under a combination of heat and pressure that makes it behave in a plastic way. In this context, 'plastic' is not referring to the material used to make children's toys, but to the way that some solid materials flow, even though they are not molten. Toffee seems solid, but if left long enough will lose its shape. Tarmac on roads

does the same. So the rocks under the surface seem solid in the short term, but in the long term can creep and flow.

In the 1960s, an elegant theory came together that would change the science of geology for ever, and completely alter the way we see the world. The theory of *plate tectonics* was born. Scientists realized that the Earth's surface is like a giant jigsaw, made up of six large pieces – plates – and several smaller ones; and these plates are all in motion.

The Himalayas, created when two tectonic plates collided and crumpled

For some time, anyone contemplating an atlas of the world saw that the east coast of South America and the west coast of Africa looked as if they would fit each other like jigsaw pieces if they were drawn together. Not only did the plate tectonics theory explain that they once did exactly that, it also explained many other puzzling patterns of volcanoes and earthquakes.

These huge plates, with the continents riding on top as passengers, move around the globe at a rate of several centimetres a year; in some places the plates collide, and in other places they pull apart.

Where two plates meet, one of two things can happen, depending on the nature of the edge of the colliding plates. The Earth's crust under the continents is thick, up to 40 km (25 miles) in places, but the continents themselves are relatively light in weight. The crust under the oceans is much

The early atmosphere, a deadly cocktail of toxic greenhouse gases

thinner, only 3–5 km (2–3 miles) in places, but is much heavier. If two continents collide, they simply crumple up, forming mountain chains like the Himalayas. But if continental crust meets oceanic crust, the heavier oceanic crust slides *under* the continental crust, or is *subducted*. This creates long, very deep ocean trenches, like the Marinas trench which is 11 km (7 miles) deep. But as the oceanic crust graunches under the continental crust, it creates earthquakes, and as the oceanic rock is forced downwards the increasing pressure melts the rocks. Where this molten rock forces its way to the surface, it creates volcanoes. All round the Pacific Ocean, the 'ring of fire' is a pattern of earthquakes and volcanoes at subduction zones, formed by a complex pattern of plate collisions.

Where two plates pull apart, the landscape is equally dramatic. New rock must well up to fill the gap; on land this is happening in Africa along the famous Great Rift Valley. Again this disruption creates volcanoes as molten rock – magma – flows up from the interior to erupt as lava.

Volcanoes played a crucial part in the history of the early Earth. They belched out gases that, over time, created a primitive atmosphere. It was not an atmosphere that we could breathe – one breath of this deadly cocktail of carbon dioxide, methane and nitrogen would kill us. Some of these gases – carbon dioxide, water vapour – acted as *greenhouse gases*. These particular gases trap the sun's heat near the surface, something like a greenhouse, so the planet gets hotter and hotter. The early Earth may even have had temperatures as high as 80°C (176°F); too hot for us to tolerate.

But at this temperature something happens, something that may make Planet Earth unique. Among the range of temperatures that exist in the galaxy, from absolute zero to thousands of degrees, the average temperature of planet Earth is usually in the range 0–100°C (32–212°F). And at *these* temperatures something special happens – water exists as a liquid. Any hotter and the water would boil away, hanging in the atmosphere as water vapour; any colder and it would freeze solid as ice. *This* is why Earth is unique, why its position in the solar system – not too near the sun, not too far away – allows water to form oceans, rivers, streams and rain. And almost as soon as there was liquid water, there was life

The Changing Magnet

The Earth's magnetic field not only changes the position of the magnetic poles, but many times in the Earth's history it has completely reversed its direction; the North Pole and South Pole have switched over.

How do we know this? From the rocks, the fragments of the planet that carry the story of the Earth. When molten rock from a volcano cools, it forms an igneous rock, like basalt for example; this rock has grains of a magnetic mineral called magnetite. But as it cools the grains of *magnetite* behave something like tiny magnets, and line themselves up with the Earth's magnetic field. Once the rock has solidified, the grains of magnetite are fixed, and so have kept a record of the Earth's magnetic field at the time the rock was formed. This property is called *remanent magnetism*.

In 1968, the Research Vehicle *Glomar Challenger* was used to survey the ocean floor; adapting techniques that were used for finding petroleum deposits, the crew could take drill-core samples from the ocean floor.

The magnetic field in the rocks of the sea floor had been surveyed in the 1950s using a sensitive magnetometer, developed to identify submarines. They found that the basalt of the seabed had startling variations

rock cools and is magnetized in 'normal' polarity

rock cools and is magnetized in 'reverse' polarity

mirror image of other side

rock cools as it moves away

magma rising from interior

plates pulling apart

The spreading ridge and the Earth's changing magnetism

in their remanent magnetism. Some basalt lined up with the Earth's magnetic field as it is now, called normal polarity, but other rock seemed to be the other way round, as if it had formed by lining up with a magnetic field that was reversed. And the different types of magnetic rock formed a pattern of stripes.

The *Glomar Challenger* spent a year crossing back and forth over the Atlantic Ocean, taking drill-core samples at different locations. From these samples, they could find the age of the rocks. Matching these up with the pattern of stripes that had been found in the magnetic properties of the rocks, the scientists found that the rocks were youngest at the centre of the mid-ocean ridge and were progressively older moving away either side of the ridge. Also, the patterns were mirror images of each other, with the line of reflection again down the centre of the ridge.

They realized that new rock was being produced at the centre of the ridge, and moved away either side, like a conveyor belt, at a rate of a few centimetres a year. The whole Atlantic Ocean is expanding. And the magnetic records in this rock showed that the Earth's magnetic field had switched over – the North Pole becoming the South Pole, and vice versa – 22 times in the last 4.5 million years.

chapter 3 Life

Life is an offensive, directed against the repetitious

mechanism of the Universe.

Alfred North Whitehead

The early Earth, with its toxic atmosphere, was as lifeless as the other planets in the solar system. Yet something happened, something changed. There was a time when the planet was dead, and then, suddenly, there was life.

Why Earth? What made the difference between this planet and the others that we know about?

The answer is liquid water.

All the chemistry of life *must* take place in a solution of liquid water; the presence of water is a fundamental requirement for life as we know it. And the basic building block of all life is a special molecule, which has all the properties that make life the way it is. Its full name is *deoxyribose nucleic acid*, but it is usually known as DNA. The DNA molecule is made up from basic elements found everywhere in the universe – hydrogen, carbon, nitrogen, oxygen and a few others – but it is the *way* these are combined that makes DNA the complex, beautiful and delicate structure it is.

The molecule is a very, very long strand of four units, repeating over and over again. It is rather like a word, made up from only four letters, but that can repeat as often as needed – and the word is over a million letters long. But

All life depends on liquid water

**The double helix
structure of DNA**

the pattern of these four repeating units carries the information that tells a bacterium it is a bacterium, a mouse it is a mouse, an oak tree it is an oak tree, and so on. In humans, this pattern tells us we *are* human, but it also tells us whether we might be a blue-eyed blonde or a sultry brunette, whether we will be tall or short, colour-blind, prone to certain diseases – it makes us the unique individuals we are.

DNA not only carries the information in its repeating pattern, but it replicates itself, and this is another key to life, the ability to reproduce, making copies of the original. Orange trees make orange trees, mice make more mice, and this does not vary. The reason DNA can do this is in its structure; it is made of two 'threads', two chains twisted together so that they form a double helix. Under certain conditions, they can unzip themselves into separate chains and then grow new ones, so one molecule can reproduce to create two.

Sometimes, during this process, a mistake can creep in. One mistake in a million may not seem relevant, but when a mistake is made the new molecules will be slightly different from the original. And this is what gives life its variety; as a new generation brings a new feature, life evolves. Over hundreds of millions of years, evolution has created a staggering diversity of life, from bacteria to whales.

Where did all this life come from? How did DNA come into being in the first place? This is the ultimate question. In the 1950s, a famous experiment by Miller and Urey in the University of Chicago simulated the conditions that were thought to exist on the early Earth. An electric spark, to simulate lightning, was passed through a mixture of gases that represented the Earth's atmosphere; the chemical reaction produced amino acids, the building blocks of organic molecules, the molecules of life.

But they were still inert, lifeless, a long way from the living properties of the DNA molecule. How this crucial step occurred is still not clear. There are various theories about how different organic molecules could have combined in a primaeval warm 'soup', eventually generating life. Some even think that the original organic molecules may have been brought to the Earth from outer space, carried here by meteors that rained down on the planet.

Wherever the first life came from, the first life on Earth was probably established by 3.9 billion years ago. It was a simple form of bacterium, just growing, reproducing and dying. Nothing else. The early Earth's atmosphere is thought to have had much more carbon dioxide than that of today, and almost no oxygen. But carbon dioxide is a potent *greenhouse gas*; it traps the sun's heat at the surface, so the early Earth was much hotter than it is now. Some think it could have been 80°C (176°F) or higher, and that the water in the oceans would have been hot. The bacteria were *anaerobic*, meaning they lived without oxygen, and they thrived in conditions far too hot for most life to tolerate. How do we know all this? To describe what life was like hundreds of millions of years ago may seem like speculation, but there are a few places where the conditions of early Earth still exist, and one of these places is a famous tourist attraction – Yellowstone National Park.

Yellowstone, the first national park to be created, crosses the states of northwest Wyoming, southern Montana and eastern Idaho, and welcomes more than three million visitors a year. The park is probably best known for its geysers, particularly 'Old Faithful'. Every hour or so, give or take a few minutes, a crowd of onlookers gathers along the designated viewing area, some sitting on the benches, some standing. They have come to watch a column of steam and boiling water shoot some 18 m (60 ft) into the air, in an eruption lasting for a few minutes. When the eruption is over, the people drift away and, underground, the cycle that creates the eruption begins again.

There are hundreds of geysers in Yellowstone, many higher or more dramatic than Old Faithful, but few as reliable in their timing. Hot water bubbles and boils its way to the surface to form pools and springs; steam hangs in the air, giving the park a surreal beauty. Some of the pools are of deep, strange colours, a legacy of the minerals in the water. All this activity is due to Yellowstone's position over a 'hot spot', an area of the Earth's crust where magma from deep in the planet's interior rises to within a few kilometres of the surface, lurking in a huge chamber that then heats the surrounding rocks. The surface water trickles down through the porous rocks and is heated to temperatures well above its boiling point. But the water cannot boil away because it is under immense pressure. When it does eventually find its way back to the surface, it might explode into the air, like the eruption at Old Faithful, or emerge more gently in the springs and pools. More than half a million years ago, the volcano lurking under Yellowstone erupted in an explosion that produced flows of ash, pumice and gases, sent a column of gases high into the atmosphere and created a huge crater – a caldera, nearly 80 km (50 miles) long and 50 km (30 miles) wide. But the Earth under Yellowstone is still restless, there are still earthquake tremors as the magma shifts and settles in its underground chambers.

When Yellowstone was declared a National Park in 1872, by US Congress, it was recognized as a refuge for spectacular wildlife. Buffalo wander the grassy plains, bears hide in the woods, elk drink at the rivers and streams. But in the 1960s a different form of life was found in Yellowstone; anaerobic bacteria were discovered in the hot springs, in water that was almost boiling. These were possibly the descendants of the ancient bacteria that for so long were the only life on the planet; they were certainly similar. They live in mats, of different colours, in the hot pools and springs, and flourished in these scalding waters which gives rise to their name, *thermophiles*, 'heat lovers'.

Life on Earth stayed like this for another billion years or two. And they would have stayed like this, unchanging, timeless if it hadn't been for a new life form, a different form of bacterium, that was to change the face of the Earth for ever. Instead of taking energy from minerals, this new life form made food by using the energy of sunlight to process carbon dioxide and water. This process, *photosynthesis*, is the basis for all plant life today.

Yellowstone National Park, where hot water and steam rise up from underground

Overleaf: **Primitive bacteria colour the hot springs of Yellowstone**

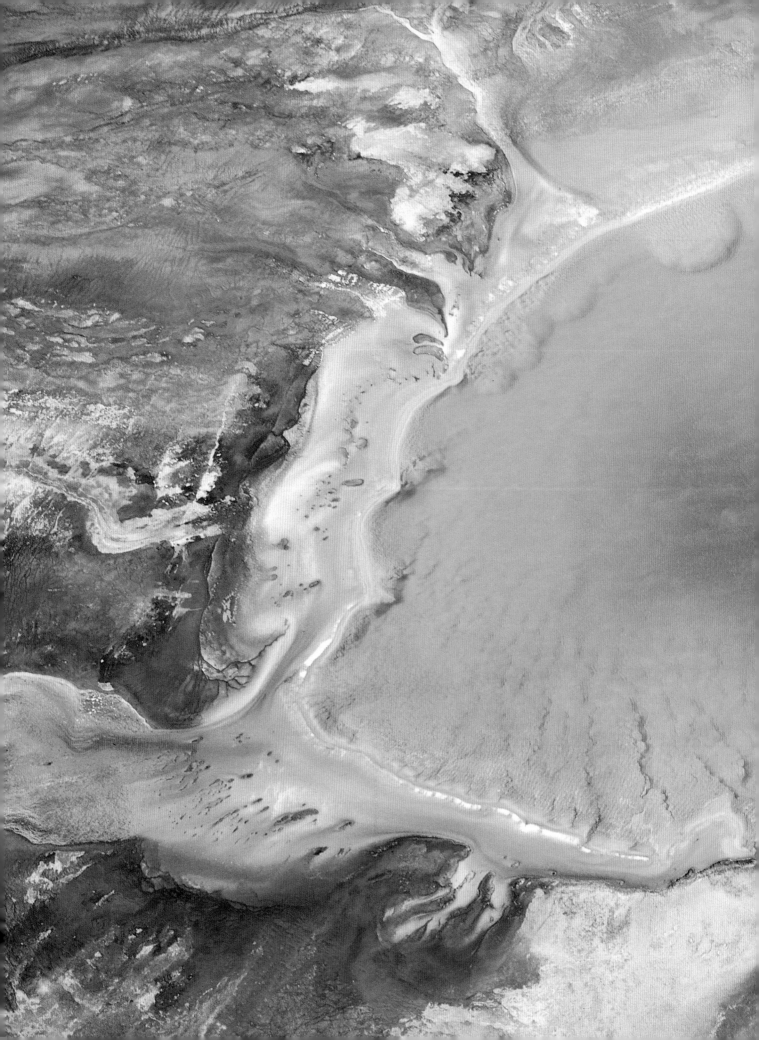

The new forms of bacteria were a blue-green colour, cyan, and are known as *cyanobacteria*. They are sometimes referred to as 'blue-green algae', but are not related to algae as we know them today; rather they were another primitive form of bacteria.

From the reaction of carbon dioxide and water, powered by sunlight, photosynthesis produces two chemicals – a form of sugar as food for the plant and a poisonous waste gas that was fatal to the ancient anaerobic bacteria that had ruled the world. Oxygen.

Until then, all the oxygen on the planet was locked in other chemical forms; the 'O' in the H_2O of water, or in chemicals that made up different minerals and rocks. But now, for the first time, it was released as a pure gas into the atmosphere. This was the worst case of global pollution the planet has ever known. As the oxygen built up, the ancient aerobic bacteria either died out or retreated to places where the deadly oxygen gas could not reach them.

This change in the Earth's atmosphere occurred roughly two billion years ago, over a period of a few hundred million years. If the Earth is four and a half billion years old, then nearly half its history had passed, with nothing but the ancient bacteria to appreciate it. The new life forms gradually used up most of the carbon dioxide, increasing the proportion of oxygen in the atmosphere. With less carbon dioxide, there was less 'greenhouse effect' so, over time, the Earth cooled down. Most of the oxygen gas in the atmosphere consists of molecules of two oxygen atoms linked together, but there is a different kind of oxygen, made of three oxygen atoms – ozone. Ozone formed a layer in the upper atmosphere, where it acted like a blanket, protecting the surface below by absorbing harmful ultraviolet radiation. Before then, to avoid this radiation, it is possible that life may have been constrained to living in water, deep enough to absorb the radiation but shallow enough to allow light to penetrate. Oxygen altered the way that light was absorbed and scattered in the atmosphere – it changed the sky to blue.

So the first life forms could not live in the presence of oxygen, and the next life forms produced oxygen as a waste product; yet now animal life as we know it depends on oxygen. But oxygen *is* a poisonous gas – as deadly to us as it is to the first anaerobic bacteria; it is just that the more recent newcomers, the animals and plants, have evolved

Most early life flourished in the warm shallow water of the oceans

Oxygen and Fire

For the first three billion years of the Earth's history – about two-thirds of the time that it has existed – there was no oxygen in the atmosphere. It took millions of years for the life forms called cyanobacteria to produce free oxygen gas as a waste product – oxygen that was to change the atmosphere and the Earth forever. Because where there is oxygen there is fire.

Fire is the fast burning of a material that produces heat and light. And fire feeds on oxygen which, in most cases, it gets from the air. Long before humans learned to control fire, it occurred naturally through the action of lightning. And all round the world an ecology evolved to make use of fire; as the undergrowth burned away, new plant life could grow quickly in the fertile ash left behind. In some cases, such as in long-leaf pine forests, the seed does not germinate until it has been burned, so that the ground would be cleared of competition.

Humans did not discover how to create fire for themselves until about 7000 BC, either striking a flint to produce a spark, or by rubbing two pieces of wood together until friction heats the surrounding kindling enough for it to light. Our ancestors used fire

Fire is a natural part of the ecology of the forest

to provide warmth and light, to heat and cook their food, and to keep predators away. They learned that they could clear forests of undergrowth, which encouraged fresh growth to attract game animals. By burning forests in this way, they could grow crops in the fertile ash left behind, in a method known as *slash-and-burn* agriculture.

Eventually, the ability to control fire was the crucial step in the development of tech-

nology. At first, it was used to heat clay to make pottery, or to melt metallic ore, but as our technology advanced the underlying power came from the control of fire; fire brings the heat and light of the sun down to Earth. It is the most volatile of the four classical elements, and in most early cultures was seen as a living entity. It moves, it grows, it dances, it can be the tiny glimmer of a flame or a roaring inferno.

ways of disarming the deadly molecules. They evolved chemicals in their cells that combine with the oxygen and escort it safely in and out of the cell. But oxygen still does some damage. It is highly reactive, so it breaks down vital cell chemistry. It contributes to the ageing process, giving us wrinkles and stopping us from living for ever; in the quest for eternal youth, people buy anti-oxidants, to mop up rogue oxygen.

We cannot live without oxygen, and it kills us in the end. So why do we bother with it? Because it gives us energy. Aerobic respiration, using oxygen, is a very efficient, controlled burning of sugars. Glucose reacts with oxygen and the breakdown products are carbon dioxide, water and lots of energy – far more than could be produced by the ancient, anaerobic bacteria.

A crucial period in the development of life started about 540 million years ago, yet this is recent compared to the Earth's history. By now, four-fifths of the planet's story has

passed. But during the Cambrian period, which lasted until 500 million years ago, life on the planet changed irrevocably. Over the previous few billion years, all life consisted of single-celled creatures, simple basic units of life. But now, creatures arose that were more complex, whose bodies were made of multiple cells, and these cells took on different functions: some cells could sense the surroundings, became eyes, ears; some cells formed a gut, primitive nervous systems, muscles. Minerals were used to make hard parts such as shells, and for the first time, when these creatures died, they left their signatures as recognizable fossils.

There was a dramatic increase in the number of different life forms. An explosion of evolution over a few million years gave rise to all the types of body plans of creatures on Earth that there would ever be. Nothing radically new has evolved since then, just adaptations of a few dozen basic blueprints.

This dramatic increase in the different forms of life took

place within a relatively short period of time compared to the Earth's history – only a few million years. Because this increase took place in the Cambrian period, it is sometimes referred to as the 'Cambrian Explosion'. From that time on, animals and plants that died left a legacy of fossils that help geologists and palaeontologists piece together their history.

Until then, there was no life on land to speak of, other than possibly some of the bacteria. Life had settled in the shallow water at the edges of the oceans. But by about 420 million years ago the first plants had appeared on land; they ranged from small mosses to giant tree ferns, all living by photosynthesis, all releasing yet more oxygen into the atmosphere. Only ten million years later, animals followed. The first creatures on land were air-breathing fish, and *arthropods*, creatures with jointed legs – the ancestors of spiders, insects and crabs.

By 345 million years ago, winged insects had taken to the air, and the first reptiles walked the land. All the continents were joined together, forming one huge landmass, and the climate was getting warmer. We are now reaching the Jurassic period, 200 million years ago, when the Earth was ruled by the dinosaurs, and the first true birds appeared. There *were* mammals by then, but they were small, insignificant, shrew-like creatures. But then, 65 million years ago, something happened, something that changed the course of life on Earth. For some reason, there was a mass extinction and the dinosaurs disappeared. It was probably due to a dramatic change in the climate, a cooling that may have been due to a comet colliding with the Earth; no one knows for sure. The result, however, was that as the dinosaurs disappeared, mammals could evolve, developing bigger brains, adapting to the climate and environment. And a mere four million years ago one type of mammal stood upright, which freed its hands to create tools, and it developed intelligence and language. The rest, as they say, is history.

Telling the story like this suggests that evolution was a process of improvement, from bacteria to humans. But in the grand scheme of things humans are an aberration, a minor hiccup in the planet's story of life. In the beginning, the planet was dominated by bacteria – and it is still. They are everywhere, from the harshest environments on the planet to the inside of our bodies, from the deepest oceans to the highest mountains. It is even possible that the number of bacteria outweighs everything else that lives on Earth. We are continually discovering bacteria that live where we could never have expected; they are even found living in the Earth's crust. Bacteria are the dominant forms of life on this planet, the great success story; they were always the life forms that would inherit the Earth.

Life in Other Worlds?

As far as we know, we are alone. We have not – yet – found any evidence of life in any other worlds. But can we narrow down the search? Are there certain conditions that we should look for, as we explore further into space?

For most of the Earth's history, life existed as a primitive bacterium, so, if an alien had visited our planet then, it would have thought that was the total of life on Earth, and apart from possibly taking a few samples would have moved on to something more interesting. At that stage, the alien would not have known that eventually the bacterium would evolve into something else.

As we search for life elsewhere, we are looking for two things: the presence of carbon, and the presence of liquid water. Carbon is a fairly common element in the galaxy, but all life is based on this one atom; it has special properties that give it a unique chemistry. It forms certain types of long chains, and it can form a molecule in the shape of a ring of six atoms, allowing other atoms to attach themselves to it in different ways. Carbon is the fundamental material of DNA.

But for the chemistry of life to happen it must happen in a solution of liquid water. So we would look for a planet, or a moon of a planet, that has – or had in the past – liquid water.

For some time, it was thought that Mars had liquid water. At the end of the nineteenth century, the dark streaks on its surface were thought to be 'canals'. Then, in 1996, a rock from Mars was thought to show evidence of fossils created by bacteria, but there was much heated discussion in academic circles, and no conclusions drawn. The Pathfinder mission in July 1997 sent back masses of new data, but still no evidence of life.

But there is somewhere else in our solar system that might be worth searching for signs of life – the fourth moon of Jupiter, an icy world called Europa. It is approximately the same size as our own moon, but its surface seems to be covered in ice. This ice is smooth, but shows straight fracture lines; fractures like this could occur if the ice was not solid, but floating on water.

The surface of Europa is freezing, as cold as –145°C (–229°F). So why has the water not frozen? Possibly because volcanic activity in the interior is keeping it warm – or because the huge tidal effect of Jupiter tugging on the waters of Europa as it orbits the giant planet is generating heat. Either way, if there is liquid water on Europa, the conditions *could* be right for life under the ice, life that does not rely on the presence of oxygen, in the same way as our ancient bacteria did not need oxygen. We have yet to explore this possibility.

chapter 4

The Gates of Hell

It looked as if the whole land was ablaze, like one big

furnace, and the sea boiled, just as a cooking pot full of

meat boils when it is well plied by fire.

The holy father comforted his monks, saying 'Soldiers of

Christ, be strengthened in faith unfeigned and in spiritual

weapons, for we are in the confines of Hell.'

The Voyage of St Brendan – *John J. O'Meara*

In the early part of the sixth century, an Irish monk, St Brendan the Navigator, set out from the west coast of Ireland in an open boat, a coracle, on a great voyage, a 'voyage for Christ'. Brendan and his 17 companions were to leave the safety of their monastery, in what is now County Kerry, and sail west in search of the 'Promised Land'. Brendan was an experienced sailor, he had often journeyed around the coast of Ireland and Scotland visiting other monasteries, but this was the first time they were to sail into the great unknown.

Fire meets ice as a volcano erupts under the glacier Vatnajokull, 1966

A Latin version of the tale of St Brendan was known possibly as early as the ninth century, telling the story of the voyage in some detail. And in that story it tells of how they arrived at a barren, stony island, where they could hear bellows and hammers, as if giant blacksmiths were working a furnace. One of the giants appeared and threw a piece of fiery, burning rock at their boat, and suddenly the whole island was on fire. They came to a mountain that belched out smoke and fire; and the sea around the island seemed to be boiling. St Brendan was convinced they had found the gates of hell. They had probably arrived at Iceland.

Iceland itself is a young island, roughly halfway between Europe and North America in the north Atlantic

'Strokkur', one of the many geysers on Iceland

Ocean. It was created by the forces that are still active below its surface, the same forces that make Iceland the most volcanic place on Earth. From deep in the Earth's interior, a plume of molten rock, magma, rises up through the mantle and breaks through the surface, creating a hot spot.

Roughly 200 volcanoes are still active on Iceland and there is an eruption somewhere, on average, every five years. But, on a day-to-day basis, the most obvious signs of the fires under the surface are the hot springs and geysers. The word *geyser* comes from the name of the 'Great Geysir', the best known geyser in Iceland. It used to erupt regularly, but, to entertain tourists, guides started to throw soap in to reduce the surface tension and make it erupt on command. Eventually, this upset the dynamics of the geyser, so sadly it no longer erupts so dramatically. But everywhere else hot water bubbles to the surface, in mud pools, springs, or spouting, exploding jets of boiling water.

The first people to settle in Iceland were the Norwegians; in AD 874, Ingolfur Arnarson and his wife set up a home in what is now Reykjavik. Other settlers joined them, and they brought a rich tradition of storytelling – stories that told of how the world was created, and how it would end.

The great sagas tell stories of gods and heroes, of battles and love stories. But they also tell of *Ragnarok*, the end of the world. 'The sun will go dark, earth sink in the sea. From heaven, the bright stars will vanish. Steam surges and fire, flames, flicker against the very sky.'

In 1973, the people of the island of Haimey, one of the Vestmann Islands to the southwest of mainland Iceland, had their own private glimpse of *Ragnarok*. Haimey is the largest of the islands, its town, Vestmannaeyjar, a thriving fishing port. In January, violent gales in the north Atlantic forced several fishing boats to take shelter in Haimey's harbour; 70 ships came in to shelter from the storm.

In the middle of the night, on 23 January, a violent eruption surprised everyone. Although there had been a swarm of earthquakes – a series of small, repeating tremors – on the night of 21 January, without a full network of sensors in place it was impossible to find the source of the tremors. It was likely that they were coming from the nearby Katla volcano, which was still active.

But at two o'clock in the morning of the 23rd, a fissure opened up, some 1.6 km (1 mile) long, and it was only 200 m (650 ft) from the edge of the town of Vestmannaeyjar. Forty or so fountains of lava shot into the air, but the fissure was on land that was sloping away from the town, so the lava could run away from the nearby houses. A light wind blew any tephra – burning ash and fragments of rock – away from the town. The extra ships in the harbour could evacuate the town people to the Icelandic mainland.

Before long, though, the wind changed direction, blowing the tephra over the town; some of the houses were burned, some were buried under the fine volcanic ash, collapsing under its thickness. A month later, the new crater collapsed in the direction of the town, lava flowed towards the harbour and the situation was suddenly much more serious. But the volunteers fought back.

In a valiant attempt to stop the lava from completely destroying the harbour, they quickly organized a system of pumps to spray the lava with seawater. If they could cool the lava down enough, it would start to solidify and slow down. It might even stop altogether. Initially, the lava was so runny that the water did not seem to make any difference.

'Blue lagoon', created by warm waste water from a thermal power plant

Overleaf: **The myth of *Ragnarok*, when the world will end in smoke and fire**

The Voyage of the Navigator

Brendan's story was written down possibly in the ninth century, as a Latin translation of an Irish epic poem. It told how the monk and priest, Brendan, took some of his brothers in a boat out into the open sea, sailing on a voyage to find the fabled 'Promised Land of the Saints'. Although it is similar to other ancient Irish epics that tell of great voyages, some aspects of Brendan's story imply that it could have been based on a real event.

He was born in what is now Tralee, in County Kerry, in about AD 484. He grew up to become a monk, eventually establishing his own monasteries in Ireland and Scotland. An accomplished sailor, he often travelled from Ireland around Scotland and as far as France in a coracle, an open boat.

But his great voyage was to take him out into the Atlantic Ocean. With his 17 companions he built a new boat, with a mast and sail, and stocked it with enough provisions for 40 days.

They sailed west, and the story tells of the many and strange islands they visited. At an abandoned island, they were fed and given shelter; another they found was covered in birds, and at yet another, there were giant sheep.

Among the islands they visited, one had dark, steep, slippery sides; when they finally landed on the island, they found it moved. In fact, it was a huge whale, and Brendan had

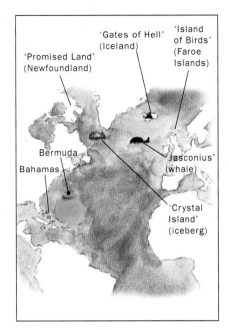

Possible correspondence of places visited by St Brendan

a vision in which God told him it was called Jasconius.

The boat came to a crystal pillar, a huge tower they thought was made of white marble. The boat could pass through openings in the pillar, and they could sail around it; this is an accurate description of an iceberg. Then they sailed to the land of fire and boiling seas, the gates of hell themselves; this could have been Iceland, when a volcano was erupting.

When they finally reached the island that they thought was the Promised Land they had sought for so long, it was surrounded in a thick fog. They were told that they had not been able to find the island for so long because God wanted to show them first the secrets of the great ocean. They had finally completed their voyage, and could now return home, to tell of their strange and wonderful adventures.

In the 1970s, Tim Severin built a replica of Brendan's boat, and retraced a possible route for his journey. It took him a year to cross the north Atlantic, but he arrived safely in Newfoundland, and the shores of Newfoundland are notorious for their fog. Certainly it was possible for Brendan and his crew to travel such distances, and it may be that they made landfall on the shores of America, a thousand years before Columbus' historic arrival.

But as the pumping system became more elaborate, and they could take the water closer to the source of the lava, the lava's relentless progress was halted.

With hindsight, it is difficult to say how much difference the seawater made, as the lava flow may have slowed down naturally, but the attempt to fight the force of the volcano was watched the world over. Living on a volcanically active area may seem hazardous, but does have its advantages. Iceland has access to unlimited cheap, clean energy.

The island is crisscrossed by rivers, many of which fall over waterfalls as they cut their way through the young rock. They provide more than enough energy for the island's power needs; only about 7 per cent of the potential hydroelectric power is actually utilized. And there is also a source of direct energy, the hot water that bubbles up from underground. Rainwater – or glacier melt – that seeps down through the porous rock is heated by the hot rock just below the surface, and is forced back up to the surface, boiling or near boiling. This hot water is pumped directly round the homes to provide central heating; over 85 per cent of the homes in the capital, Reykjavik, are heated in this way.

When Arnarson, the Viking, first arrived in Reykjavik, he named it the 'bay of smoke', as the volcanoes left plumes of ash and dust hanging in the air. Now, 1,200 years later, Reykjavik is referred to as the 'smokeless city'. Iceland's most important source of income is fishing and fish processing. Its position in the north Atlantic is ideal as a base for the fishing boats, and its low-cost energy supports the processing plants where the fish are treated for export. Heated greenhouses support the growing of exotic fruit and

Waterfalls and rivers cross Iceland, driving the many hydroelectric power stations

vegetables all year round, and the outlets from the power plant provide warm outdoor bathing pools throughout summer and winter.

The island of fire is also a land of ice. The Vatnajokull glacier is Europe's biggest icecap; it has an area larger than all the glaciers in continental Europe combined. On the surface it seems stable, even peaceful. But in 1996 all that was to change. For some time there were signals that something was about to happen, but these warnings grumbled on for a year. Earth tremors – swarms of earthquakes – implied that something was happening deep underground, that somewhere magma was on the move.

Then, on 10 September 1996, the seismographic equipment picked up some more activity under the ice, and the next morning a huge indentation had appeared in the ice, 100 m (330 ft) deep. This was to be the only sign that underneath, out of sight, an eruption had started 600 m (2,000 ft) below the surface. The eruption was melting the ice, and the water flowing under the ice formed a channel that stretched to Lake Grimsvotn, a lake under Vatnajokull some 15 km (9 miles) away. Lake Grimsvotn is a lake under the ice, over a caldera formed by previous volcanic eruptions. The water in this lake does not freeze, as it is over a warm geothermal area; and the water from the eruption also flowed into the lake, forcing the ice above it to rise.

Finally, on 2 October, the eruption broke through the icecap, creating a column of ash, and the next day a series of huge eruptions hurled tephra 300 m (1,000 ft) into the air. In the violence of the eruption, lightning flashed in the billowing clouds of ash. Once the weather cleared, on 12 October, it revealed a huge gorge, hundreds of metres wide, with the surface of the water now 300 m (1,000 ft) below the top of the gorge. The eruption roared for two weeks before subsiding.

But something was missing. It was inevitable that an eruption of this power would melt a vast amount of ice, which in turn would create a *jokulhlaup*, a sudden flood created by a melted glacier. Yet the flood that was expected had not appeared, and scientists, photographers and journalists waiting patiently to witness the flood were disappointed. They waited for days and then waited for weeks, and still nothing happened.

It was not until the morning of 5 November that the *jokulhlaup* finally escaped. Nearly 4 km³ (1 cubic mile) of water burst free, in a huge flood that swept away bridges, destroyed power lines and carried huge blocks of ice and rock, 9 m (30 ft) high, in its path. There was no loss of life, but over 15 million US dollars' worth of damage, to be carried by Iceland's population of only 265,000.

Iceland's position in the north Atlantic Ocean is directly above a spreading ridge; it is a gateway to a tear in the ocean floor where Europe and America are pulling away from each other, at about the rate that fingernails grow. Most of this ridge is unseen, running down the centre of the Atlantic, only poking above the surface at Iceland and at a few islands like Tristan De Cunha. The activity of the spreading ridge normally occurs under 5 km (3 miles) of water, but Iceland has been pushed to the surface by the volcanic hot spot. Here, the processes that created the Earth are still happening. Volcanoes erupt, new land is created; the fires of the Earth are close to the surface.

There is a basic assumption made in the study of the Earth's geology that might seem obvious, but needs stating. It's the theory of uniformitarianism, a clumsy word for the simple idea that the forces and processes that created the early Earth are the same forces and processes that operate today. Or, put the other way round, by studying the activity that goes on today we can find out more about how the early Earth was formed. At Iceland we can witness, first hand, some of the processes that created our world four and a half billion years ago.

Where two plates pull apart under the ocean, as if tearing the fabric of the seabed apart, new molten rock wells up along the rip, cooling as it meets the cold seawater. As this new rock – basalt – cools, it stacks up, so a double ridge is formed along the tear. Like a global conveyor belt, new ocean floor is created at these 'spreading ridges'; it is carried away by the moving plates and is finally destroyed, plunging under another plate at the subduction zones some 600 million years later. On the continents, rocks have been found that are billions of years old, but on the ocean floor there are no rocks older than 600 million years.

A spreading oceanic ridge is a place of wonder and mystery, a place where humans have, at best, snatched glimpses of this hidden world. Like all the spreading ridges, the mid-Atlantic ridge is a place we hardly know; we only discovered the activity down there a matter of decades ago. So to go on a voyage to the underworld, deep below the surface of the Atlantic, takes us into a world where *we* are the aliens.

Five km (3 miles) down, the water is nearly freezing, and pitch dark. For centuries, it was assumed that the deep sea floor was a desert, devoid of life and of little interest. This century, the two world wars saw an improvement in the technology to investigate the sea floor. And, with the

Life – But Not As We Know It

The discovery of deep sea vents at the areas of the ocean where the sea floor is splitting open, was as much of a shock to biologists as it was to geologists. Until then, it was thought that the deep seabed was a desert, too dark and too cold for anything interesting to happen.

But here, several kilometres below the surface of the ocean, the activity of the underwater volcanoes does strange things to seawater. It seeps down through a crack in the rocks of the seabed, and is heated by the molten rock, expands and is forced back to the surface of the seabed, dissolving minerals as it goes. Then it bursts back into the cold seawater at a temperature of 175°C (350°F); it does not boil because the pressure is so great at this depth. The sudden cooling causes the minerals to come out of solution, colouring the water black – creating a 'black smoker'.

This water is so toxic that if a factory was to discharge anything like it into the sea it would be prosecuted under every pollution law there is. But at these super-heated, mineral-laden black smokers whole communities live out their lives without any contact with sunlight.

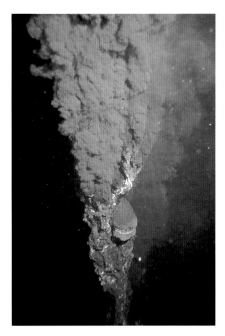

Black smoker – superheated water escapes from a crack in the seabed

Ultimately, just about every other form of life on the planet relies on sunlight at some part of its food chain. But here the energy comes from bacteria that get their energy from processing the minerals in the water. In the Pacific Ocean, at spreading ridges, huge gardens of tube worms, up to 1 m (3 ft) in length, live off these bacteria, which reside in the inside of the tubes themselves, close to the minerals from the vents.

In the Atlantic Ocean, colonies of shrimps, a few centimetres long, also live off the bacteria at the vents. Cindy Lee Van Dover, a scientist studying the vents, brought some shrimps to the surface, and in the spirit of true adventure cooked one to find out how it tasted. The result was not encouraging for potential deep-sea gourmets.

But the existence of life at these deep-sea vents has prompted a whole new set of questions about the origins of life. Could *this* be where all life on Earth began? Could these simple, primitive bacteria be the start of life as we know it?

The question is still open to speculation. Then, in the 1980s, there was another surprise. At some of the deep-sea vents, scientists found a dim glow of light. It is so dim that it needs to be measured with special instruments, and no one yet knows what is creating the light. But – in theory – where there is light, there *could* be photosynthesis. It is still only an intriguing theory, yet it is possible that not only did life originate here but this could also give a clue as to how photosynthesis began.

---

cold war of the 1960s, the threat carried by submarines triggered a massive investment in the instrumentation to detect underwater objects. All this activity resulted in the discovery of an underwater chain of mountains running down the centre of the Atlantic Ocean. If we could see the whole world without its covering of water, we would see this mountain range continue round the globe like the seams on a baseball.

Once it was realized that *this* was where new sea floor was created, it was suspected that there would be volcanic activity and hot springs. But it was not until 1974 that the submersible *Alvin*, operated by Woods Hole Oceanographic Institution, together with the French diving saucer *Cyane* and the French bathyscape *Archimede*, explored the mid-oceanic ridge for the first time.

Not only did they confirm that molten rock was emerging through the tear in the sea floor, but something very

strange was happening. Wherever a spreading ridge was explored, huge vents, *black smokers*, were found. Seawater, seeping down through the cracks in the seabed, was heated by the hot rocks below the surface and erupted out into the cold sea at temperatures often higher than 300°C (572°F). The intense pressure at these depths stopped the water from boiling, and minerals in the water coloured it black.

And even more of a surprise – there was life here. In the Atlantic, there are massive colonies of shrimps, 5 cm (2 in) long, feeding off bacteria. The bacteria's energy comes from the minerals in the water, the shrimps' energy comes from the bacteria. At black smokers throughout the oceans, these strange communities, based on bacteria, live in total darkness, a bizarre form of life that does not depend on sunlight in any way.

The light from the submersible may have been the first light that this world had *ever* experienced.

PART TWO
WIND AND WATER

chapter 5

Water from the Sky

I am the daughter of Earth and Water,

And the nursling of the sky.

I pass through the pores of the ocean and shores;

I change but I cannot die.

'The Cloud' — Percy Bysshe Shelley

For all we know, the Earth could be unique, in that it rains here. The liquid water on the planet is part of a huge cycle, moving from the sea to the clouds, falling as rain to the ground, flowing down the rivers back to the sea. And all this can only happen *because* water exists as a liquid. Most of the planet's water – 99 per cent – is held in the oceans, and the rest is continually in motion as part of the cycle. The water that is held by the atmosphere is a critical part of our weather.

Water can exist as a solid, a liquid or a gas. Most of the water in the solar system, if not the galaxy, is locked up in the form of ice, and it stays that way for thousands of years. As we have seen, water can exist as a liquid within the tiny range of 1–100°C (32–212°F), and this is the liquid that sustains life, that determines the nature of the Earth.

As gas, water vapour is invisible, its presence in the atmosphere felt rather than seen. The amount of water vapour in the air around us depends on the temperature and pressure of that air. We are familiar with hot, humid days, when our sweat doesn't evaporate and everything feels damp and sticky; at this time, the air already holds as much water vapour as it can, and will accept no more. The warmer the air, or the higher the pressure, or both, the more water vapour it will hold.

The water in the atmosphere becomes visible when it condenses to form clouds. To see how this works, the simple act of boiling a kettle can give some clues. As the water boils, the air inside is forced out through the spout; it has been heated by the water and carries a lot of water vapour. Coming out of the spout, the water vapour is invisible, but as it rises away from the kettle the air quickly cools and cannot hold all of it. When this water vapour condenses to a liquid, it forms tiny droplets that are light enough to hang in the air and we see them as steam.

But water vapour cannot condense without something to condense on. We know how water vapour condenses on the inside of a window during a cold night, or on the outside of a cold beer bottle on a warm day. To form steam – or, more importantly, clouds – there must be something in the air. Microscopic particles act as *condensation nuclei,* and these can be minute particles of dust, or smoke, or crystals. They get into the air from volcanoes, forest fires, or tiny salt crystals from the evaporation of seawater. Without any condensation nuclei, the air can be saturated with water vapour but cannot form clouds.

The world's climate works in a similar way, but, instead of a kettle element, the system is driven by the sun. The amount of sunlight that reaches the surface of the Earth depends on where on the planet we are. The sun burns most fiercely around the equator, and as it does, it warms up the oceans. Two things happen; the air over the ocean also warms up, and the water in the sea evaporates, so the warm air holds a lot of water vapour. But warm air rises. And as this air rises it moves away from the warm water and begins to cool. Again, it cannot hold as much water vapour so the vapour condenses to form clouds.

If the droplets of water stay small enough, they just hang in the air, but if the droplets get big enough, they become too heavy and fall from the sky – as rain. Within a cloud, raindrops might condense on ice crystals, which then melt as they fall through warmer air; alternatively, small droplets in the cloud might condense on a bigger raindrop falling past them. The smallest droplets become rain when they reach 0.5 mm (⅟₅₀ in) in diameter, but they can be up to 3 mm (⅟₁₀ in) across. The bigger the drops, the faster they fall, but the larger drops tend to be flattened – like pennies – then break up as they fall to the ground.

When the wet warm air blows over land, the air is forced further upwards and is cooled even more. This creates a lot of rain – and rainforest. All round the equator, in the combination of warmth and rain, there is a belt of tropical rainforest. The belt is almost continuous on land, except for east Africa (Kenya and Tanzania) and the land to the west of the Andes (Ecuador).

In the rainforest, nature runs riot. There is no cold winter, no extreme drought, just continuous heat. The length of daylight is more or less constant, there is unlimited water. More than 2,500 mm (100 in) of rain a year fall on some rainforests and there are only two seasons – 'wet' and 'not quite so wet'. Like a well-tended greenhouse, these conditions allow plants to grow continually, with no need to die back in winter and regrow in spring, or survive otherwise harsh conditions like drought.

The tropical rainforests are crucial for the role they play in the planet's life. To put some figures to this, tropical rain-

Water droplets hang in the air as mist and cloud

forest occupies 7 per cent of the Earth's land surface, but it supports over 50 per cent of the world's different species. It is guessed that in the rainforests there are more than one and a half million species of plants and animals, many of which have never been seen by human eyes, let alone named and classified.

A typical tropical rainforest has a three-dimensional structure, with four distinct vertical layers. Different plants grow to different layers and a variety of different animals feed on the different plants. Flying over a rainforest gives a view of a dense, solid cover of the tops of the trees, the *canopy*. There is no glimpse of the secret world that lies underneath. The highest trees tower, exposed, above the canopy layer; mahogany and kapok are widely spaced, tall and strong. They receive the most intense sunlight and heat, and are strong enough to resist the wind that blows continually at this height.

Clustered below them, bunched together, are the trees that form the canopy itself, the thick layer of greenery that blocks anything below it from the sun, but also protects from the wind. But trees of the same species do not grow together, there is too much competition for space and light; find one particular tree and the next one of the same species will be hundreds of metres away.

Everything in the rainforest is subject to torrential rain, so these trees have waxy, waterproof leaves that are shaped with drip tips, so that rainwater can run straight off. Otherwise, in the warm dampness, fungal infections could set in. The canopy absorbs most of the rain that falls, but a big rainforest creates its own climate; the plants absorb the water from the soil and evaporate it through their leaves, bringing more moisture to the already wet conditions. Rainforest actually creates rain, which is why the amount of rainfall decreases when rainforest is cleared; once a rainforest has gone it can never be recreated, because the climate will have changed.

This air is humid, it holds almost as much moisture as it can; a combination of the rain, of the warm air and the evaporation of water vapour from the leaves drives the humidity up to 90–100 per cent. Under the canopy there is

**World distribution of
tropical rainforest**

no wind, so the plants disperse their seeds in other ways, such as being carried by animals. It is dark here, as most of the sunlight has been blocked by the canopy, but the temperature is fairly constant, at about 27°C (80°F). This is the *understorey*, where plants are spaced widely apart in an attempt to make use of any sunlight that does filter through. Some plants, like mimosa, rotate their leaves during the period of daylight, to follow the sun.

On the dark forest floor there is little soil, as any fallen leaves or dead animals decompose quickly in the heat. The trunks and stems of all the other plants leave little room; the plants that do grow here have to make the most of any light that reaches them, so their leaves form patterns whereby the leaves above do not shade the leaves underneath. With such little space, life wastes nothing. Some plants do not need the forest floor at all, they simply live on other plants; climbers such as the familiar 'Swiss cheese' plant grow on other trees, and epiphytes such as orchids live without any contact with the ground.

Rainforest in southeast Asia is created by the monsoons, the seasonal winds that blow in opposite directions in the different seasons. In the Indian Ocean, from October to April, the wind blows from the northeast, but from April to October it blows from the southwest. This wind, referred to as the monsoon, blows over the sea and brings torrential rain to India and southeast Asia. Enough rain falls that it sustains a rainforest, even though the seasons are more defined than in other rainforest regions.

But the biggest rainforest of them all is the Amazon jungle. It stretches more or less across the entire continent of South America. It is drained by the Amazon river, but so much rain falls on this rainforest in the wet season – January to June – that even this mighty river cannot drain it all, so some of the forest floods. The trees and plants here are used to being submerged in a metre or so of fresh water for months at a time. So much so that some of the trees have

**Tropical rainforest is created by the combination
of warmth and rain**

their seeds dispersed by fish; the pacu fish is a relative of the infamous piranha, but eats fruit instead of meat.

For the people that live in the rainforest, rain is everything to their lives. Like many cultures living with extremes of weather or natural forces, these forces take on an identity, become a living entity, a god or goddess. Rainforest stretches all through Central America, and here the great civilization of the Maya ruled for centuries. From about AD 300 to 900, they lived in their great cities, building huge stone pyramids as part of their temple complexes. They needed rain to water their crops and it would seem that rain should not be a problem to a people living in a rainforest. But it is not that simple. The right amount of rain and the right sort of rain must fall at the right time; harsh heavy rain on delicate new crops can destroy them or wash them away, and the rains need to coincide with the planting and harvesting season.

Carvings of the rain-god Chac adorn this Mayan temple wall

Rain, for the Maya people, was represented by the god Chac, a god who presided over water and rain, but who also wielded the weapon of lightning. The relationship between rain and crops is so strong that Chac is credited with opening the great rock which contained maize, the life-giving food of the people. Chac had the power to bring life or take it away by controlling the rainfall, and he was so powerful that human sacrifices were made to honour him. He was worshipped in different forms for over a thousand years.

The Maya were a peaceful people, and when, over time, their lands were invaded by the Toltecs from the north, they absorbed the new ideas and culture. But the Maya and Toltecs were in decline when the warriors of the Aztecs migrated south, into what is now Mexico. For the Aztecs,

People of the Rainforest

Deep in the heart of the Amazon rainforest, people have lived out their lives for centuries, untouched by western civilization. Among them are the gentle Arara people, who lived without contact with us until the 1980s.

Their home is on the Iriri river, a tributary of the Xingu river, in turn a tributary of the Amazon itself. It would take a day in a canoe to reach them from the nearest road. But the roads are getting nearer; the building of the Trans-Amazonian highway brought white people close to their home, and by the first time they were contacted by anthropologists they were already falling prey to diseases that we shake off in days. With no previous exposure, and hence no immune response, a common cold could kill them.

Their nearest neighbours are the Kayapo, who are more warrior-like and have been in long, sometimes violent, dispute with white loggers trying to clear their part of the rainforest. The Kayapo call the Arara people the 'monkey people', for the way that they keep animals – particularly small monkeys – as pets, running freely round their villages. The children each have one as their own pet, with the monkey often spending its time sitting on the child's head.

The Arara live in villages of 50 or so people, in huts of woven vegetation. All their needs are met by the forest; they find food by hunting in the rainforest, for monkeys and game birds. The hunters sometimes cook their prey where they find it, almost to the state of charcoal, so that they carry back a lighter burden than wet, heavy meat. They also eat the fruits of the forest, and, like all the native people of the rainforests, have an unrivalled knowledge of the properties of the plants that grow there.

Because the Arara were not contacted until recently, no one has learned their language sufficiently to preserve it. It is a quiet, strange, beautiful sing-song language, and like many other native languages is in danger of disappearing for ever. Within a matter of years of their first contact, their population had halved, due to their lack of resistance to western diseases. If their culture, and their language, is lost, an extinction as dramatic as the loss of any species, then a whole wealth of knowledge will be irrevocably lost with them.

There are lessons that should have been learned by the experience of contacting Native American tribes in the last few centuries. But it seems that the same patterns are still repeated. We assume that

An Arara child with his pet monkey

they *want* to be exposed to western civilization and capitalism, to missionaries bringing the word of Jesus; we assume that they are better off with western science, medicine, technology, even clothing. Once contact has been made, it cannot be 'unmade', and the rest is inevitable. The gentle Arara people had lived without us until the 1980s, and now their culture may be lost within a matter of generations.

the rain was brought by Tlalloc, their equivalent to Chac, and, like Chac, he brought lightning and was associated with maize. So important was the rain for growing the crops, that the name 'Tlalloc' means 'He who makes things sprout'. In many representations, Tlalloc is part jaguar, and his growls are the sound of the thunder. But Tlalloc could destroy the crops as well as give them life, and he sent certain diseases, such as leprosy and rheumatism, on the people. He had a wife, a consort, Chalchiuhtlicue, a goddess of freshwater lakes and streams.

All this may seem of academic interest to us, but, today, the ancient rituals of honouring or appeasing the rain-gods is continued by the Totonac Indians of Mexico. To ask their god for rain, they perform spectacular acrobatics, to amuse and entertain him. In early June, they may do this as often as three times a day. Five men, 'voladores', in brightly coloured costumes, climb to the top of a pole, perhaps 20 m

(65 ft) high. At the very top a square frame, attached to the pole, is free to rotate, and wound round the pole, just above the frame, are four ropes. One man will stay on the small platform on the top of the pole, playing the flute, while the other four, one each side of the square frame, attach themselves by the feet to each of the ropes.

As the ceremony begins, the man on the top plays the flute, while the four others hang upside-down over the edge of the frame. The ropes unwind, the frame rotates and the four spin round and round, descending to the ground. They are falling like the rain itself, from the four directions from which Tlalloc sends the rain.

The gift of rain is part of the great cycle of water on the planet. Whether we worship rain, pray for it, dread it, grumble about it or simply delight in it, this fresh water falling from the sky creates a unique planet that sustains life in all its different forms.

chapter 6

Heat and Dust

I know what they tell you about the desert, but you mustn't
believe them. This is no deathbed. Dig down, the earth is
moist...Boulders have turned to dust here, the dust feels like
graphite. Just before the sun sets, all the colours will change.
Green will turn to blue, red to gold.

Desert Notes — Barry Lopez

In the huge circulation systems of the Earth's air masses, as with everything, what goes up must come down. The warm, wet air that was forced upwards over land, dropping its water as rain and creating rainforest, then moves away from the equator. Cut off from the warm ocean, the air cools, and, whereas hot air rises, cool air descends. Around a belt to the north and south of the equator, this descending air creates a landscape that is the opposite extreme from the rainforest.

As it moved over the continents, this air changed. It gave up most of its moisture to the rainforest belt; and, as it came down, it was compressed. This air, under higher pressure, can hold much more water vapour than air at lower pressure. Pump up a bicycle pump, to put the air under pressure, and release it suddenly – a puff of condensation appears; as the air decompresses, the pressure drops suddenly, so it can no longer hold so much water vapour.

So, back on a larger scale, with air masses and continents, the air that descends is bone dry. As it descends, rather than dropping rain onto the land, this air sucks the moisture out. Either side of the rainforest belt, to the north and south, the sinking air masses create deserts, about 1,600 km (1,000 miles) or so either side of the equator.

Many of the great deserts of the world are created by these dry air masses moving away from the equator. The Sahara of north Africa, the Thar Desert of India, the Kalahari of Africa and the Victoria Desert of Australia are all formed by this circulation of air. Others are in the *rainshadow* of huge mountain ranges; when air drops its moisture by being forced upwards over the mountains, it is then so dry that on the other side of the mountain range it creates deserts. In the Andes, in south America, the deserts east of the mountains are created by their rainshadow. Some deserts are simply so far inland that the humid air from the sea never reaches them. The Gobi Desert in central Asia is one such desert.

But in the deserts, wherever they are in the world, water is conspicuous by its absence.

A true desert has less than 250 mm (10 in) of rain a year, and 'semi-desert' is defined as having less than 400 mm (15 in) of rain per annum. And whereas the rainforests are dominated by water the deserts are dominated by wind. There are no tall trees as in rainforest to act as windbreaks, so strong winds tear across the surface, further drying out the parched ground. And, without trees to provide shade, all of the sun's heat bakes the ground; so, even if there is any moisture in the ground, it immediately evaporates in the dry wind.

Soil not held down by vegetation turns to dust as it is blown across the ground, and in places the winds strips the land down to the bare rock, the skeleton of the Earth itself. The Painted Desert, in the southwest of the USA, has been stripped down to the colourful, striated rocks that give the area its name. Pinks, reds, brown, orange, are spectacular during the day, and as the evening light catches the low, rounded hills they seem to glow. Some of the colouring

World distribution of deserts

is due to iron oxide – rust – in the soil, but the mixture of different clays and minerals adds to the variety of colours.

Deserts are places of extremes. With no clouds and no trees, there is nothing to act as insulation, to even out the temperature. During the day, the sun burns down, heating up the ground, but as the sun sets all this heat is lost and the nights can become bitterly cold. In the Gobi Desert, for example, the daytime temperature of around 25°C (78°F) can drop to –20°C (–5°F) at night. The lack of water does not necessarily mean the desert is always hot. In the winter, the Gobi Desert often experiences violent winds and blizzards, and for months at a time the average temperature is well below freezing.

These extremes of temperatures, heating and freezing the ground, eventually cause the rocks themselves to crack and flake. During the day, the sun bakes the surface of the rock, causing it to expand, and if the rock is made of layers

The Painted Desert in the American Southwest

Overleaf: **Sand is shaped by the wind into dunes at Namib Desert, Namibia**

of different minerals they may expand at different rates, making the rock crack. If water does get into the porous rock and then freezes, it expands, and can crack or split a rock. This erosion, combined with the effect of the wind, creates sand, which is carried by the wind to act as a giant sandblaster, carving the rocks into bizarre shapes. And sand itself is blown into dunes, forming waves like water frozen in time.

Whereas the rainforests are teeming with life, in comparison deserts seem empty, abandoned. But there *is* life here; in the rainforest, everything has to live with an excess of water, yet in the desert life has to find a way to survive without it. Water is the most fundamental requirement for all life, so there are two main problems with living with so little water. The first is how to obtain water; the second is not to lose what water there is.

Some deserts have a little rain every year in fairly predicable seasons, but others may go years without a downpour. When it does rain in a desert, it is often heavy, torrential rain from thunderstorms, and this drenches the surface, running off rather than soaking the ground, even causing flash floods in the normally dry waterways.

Plants adapt to the dry conditions in many different ways. The familiar cactus in the deserts of the American west is a classic example. Leaves are a problem for desert plants, as water evaporates from them, so the cactus stores water in its fleshy stem. It does have 'leaves', but these have been modified into spines, which do not lose water and also deter animals from helping themselves to the succulent plant. A cactus also has large, flat shallow roots, so that if it does rain it can absorb the rainwater before it disappears deep into the parched ground. Then, the cactus will swell up as it absorbs more of the precious water.

Plants that have leaves still reduce the water loss; some do this by closing the leaves up in the heat of the day. Others have waxy surfaces that stop water evaporating. And some plants just shut down when there is little water available to them.

There are plants that have underground bulbs or tubers that stay inert, using little water until it rains, when they become active again. Others flower and set seed when the rains come, and then the seeds stay in the soil, sometimes for years, waiting for it to rain again. A desert such as the Sonora Desert of Arizona is a riot of colour for a few weeks after the spring rains; these *ephemeral* plants have to bloom and produce seeds before the soil dries out again.

Most desert plants are low-growing, to keep out of the drying wind, so trees, as such, are rare. The welwitschia plant of the Kalahari Desert has very deep roots to reach any subterranean water. Its reputation as a survivor derives from its long life; a welwitschia plant can live for hundreds of years.

The animals of the desert also have various and ingenious ways of conserving water. Many of them are nocturnal, staying in the cool of a burrow during the hottest time of the day. Although they will drink water if it is available, it is not essential; they get the water they need from their food, whether succulent plants or the liquid in the bodies of their prey. Rodents such as the kangaroo rat or the pocket mouse have kidneys that retain water in the body, passing very concentrated urine. In fact, the kangaroo rat can go its entire life without drinking at all. Many mammals such as the jack-rabbit (a type of hare, not a true rabbit) and some desert mice have proportionally larger ears which act as radiators, getting rid of body heat. It seems that every possible trick is used.

A barrel cactus stores water in its succulent stem

Like the plants that shut down, some animals, such as ground squirrels, go into a state that is similar to hibernation. But, whereas in hibernation an animal slows its metabolism down because of the cold, in the desert the ground squirrel enters a similar state called *aestivation* when the desert gets too hot or dry. By slowing down its heart rate and breathing, it loses less water on its breath.

In deserts near the coast, such as the Namib Desert of Africa, fog is an important source of water. It condenses onto plants and is absorbed directly, or it drips down to be absorbed by the roots. But the darkling beetle climbs to the top of a ridge exposed to the fog and sticks its rear end into the air; the fog condenses onto its body and it then drinks the water.

In the hot deserts, when the sand heats up during the day, different tricks are used to keep the contact with sand down to a minimum. The sidewinder snake makes its distinctive sideways rippling movement to get across the burning ground, and a gecko in the Namib Desert raises its feet alternately off the ground to cool them down. Some darkling beetles have extra long legs to raise their bodies off the sand as they run; they dash across open sand to get from cover to cover.

The largest – and maybe the best-known – desert is the Sahara, stretching over 5,000 km (3,000 miles) across north Africa, approximately 1,600 km (1,000 miles) wide. Although the whole area is almost entirely without rain, there are underground rivers that occasionally make their way to the surface. When they do, they create an oasis, an island of greenery in the bleak landscape. The date palm grows in these naturally irrigated areas, creating the familiar image of the oasis with palm trees; a form of acacia also grows here. The Sahara region includes the Libyan Desert to the east, the driest and hottest part, with huge sand dunes 120 m (400 ft) or more in height. There is, effectively, no water at all, and very few oases. The temperature ranges from freezing at night to as much as 54°C (130°F) during the day.

There was a time, in the distant past, when the Sahara was not a desert, but a fertile area, farmed as recently as 8,000 years ago. Archaeological evidence, such as fossils, artefacts and rock paintings, imply the presence of domestic animals – cattle, sheep and goats – as well as game animals, including giraffes and antelopes. As the climate changed, and the Sahara became more arid, permanent settlements were only practical around the oases. By the third century AD, camels replaced horses for transport, and nomadic herders had the advantage over settled communities.

Of the large mammals, camels are the supreme desert creatures. They can go without drinking for days on end, storing water in the fat that makes up their humps. Whereas dehydration would kill us within days, a camel can happily lose up to 40 per cent of its bodyweight by dehydration, then drink 135 litres (30 gallons) of water in ten minutes. And a camel does not even start to sweat until the temperature reaches 40°C (104°F).

Death Valley

There is one desert where it seems that nothing should be able to live. In southern California, in 1849, a party of 30 got lost as they tried to find a short way through to the Californian gold fields. They endured two months of 'hunger, thirst and an awful silence'. Only 18 of them survived, and, as one woman looked down on the valley after her rescue, her words 'Goodbye, Death Valley' gave the desert its name.

This valley, roughly 6 km by 26 km (3¾ miles by 16 miles), is one of the harshest deserts in the world. Most of it is below sea level, including the lowest point in the western hemisphere, at 86 m (282 ft) below sea level. It is surrounded by mountains and, in the rainshadow of the Panamint mountains to the west, it has less than 50 mm (2 in) of rain a year. Temperatures reach 52°C (125°F) in the shade in the summer, and even in winter they are rarely below 21°C (70°F).

Riverbeds are signs that water once flowed freely, but now they are parched and empty, only flowing again after heavy rain. High winds whip up dust storms and sand-storms that can last for hours. Yet Death Valley has its own fish, a type of fish found nowhere else in the world. The Death Valley pupfish.

These fish live in small pools formed by springs that bring water up from under-ground, and each pool has its own unique species of fish. The water is hot, often more than 30°C (86°F), and can be several times more salty than seawater. The fish are small, between 20 and 50 mm (¾–2 in), and they feed on whatever is available, from aquatic insects, snails and eggs to the substrate of the pool, taking mouthfuls, chewing it and spitting out the remainder.

It is thought they evolved before the area became a desert, when there were lakes and free-flowing rivers, in the Pliocene era, some two million years ago. When the climate changed and the land began to dry out, these pupfish were stranded in their isolated pools, evolving into different species.

In some pools, the fish are now endan-gered; groundwater that normally supplies the springs is being used for irrigation. At Ash Meadows, the Devil's Hole pupfish lives in a pool approximately 12 m by 5 m (40 ft

The water that the Death Valley pupfish thrives in is gradually being drained away

by 16 ft). The population of a few hundred fish is protected by law; if the spring drops below a certain level, pumping of ground water must stop. But as the nearby city of Las Vegas expands, needing more and more water, it may be that these unique pupfish are living on borrowed time.

The two kinds of camel are distinguished by their humps. The Arabian camel, now only found as a domesti-cated animal, is also known as the dromedary, and has one hump, whereas the Bactrian camel is smaller, heavier and has two humps.

The Arabian camel is at home in the extreme conditions of the desert. Its mouth is tough enough to allow it to bite through the spiny defences of many succulent desert plants, and so get at the watery flesh. In a violent sandstorm, the camel's long eyelashes protect its eyes, and it can close its nostrils against the flying sand. Its nasal passages are long, and convoluted, to reabsorb moisture that it has breathed out from its lungs before the breath reaches the outside world. Splayed feet act like snowshoes on the shifting sands, and thick skin on its knee joints and on its chest allow it to rest on the burning sand. When the Arabian camel is ridden across the desert, it can cross as much as 50 km (30 miles) a day.

Although Arabian camels are no longer found in the wild, in the late 1800s, somebody had the brilliant idea of introducing them into Australia, to work in the hot deserts of the interior. But some of them escaped and there is now a feral population of thousands of camels that survive in the Australian desert as happily as they would in their native Africa.

Although we are used to thinking of deserts in terms of hot, dry places, the most extreme deserts are at the poles – *cold* and dry. In the Arctic, there is less than 250 mm (10 in) precipitation a year, and this falls as snow. In Antarctica, the 'White Desert', there is even less – 50 mm (2 in). And here, where most of the planet's fresh water is locked in the ice, there are valleys where it is so dry there is no snow or ice. It is bitterly cold, with temperatures below –90°C (–128°F) and howling winds, but with no water there is nothing to freeze and the bare ground is exposed. Snow is a luxury that occurs where there is water in the atmosphere, and, if it does fall in these polar deserts, it is as scarce as rain in the Sahara.

chapter 7

Oceans of Air

And now the Storm-blast came, and he

Was tyrannous and strong:

He struck with his o'ertaking wings,

And chased us south along.

'The Rime of the Ancient Mariner' – Samuel Taylor Coleridge

As the Earth travels round the sun, hurtling through space, spinning on its axis, it carries a blanket of air that moves with it. The atmosphere protects us from radiation and insulates us from the cold and heat of space. And, together with the ocean, it moves heat around the globe, warming up the cold places, cooling down the hot places, and making the planet a comfortable place to live.

Why does the atmosphere not drift into space? The Earth is so big that its gravity holds the gases on the surface, although very light gases, like hydrogen, do float away. The moon is smaller, its gravity weaker; so, if there had ever been an atmosphere, it would simply have escaped.

We are aware of the atmosphere because we can breathe; we experience its changes, its movement, its moods, as weather. When the atmosphere moves, we *feel* it – anything from a breeze to a gale force wind. There are times when the air *seems* calm, but across the planet the atmosphere is in a constant state of motion. The weather we experience is mostly confined to the bottom layer of the atmosphere, stretching roughly 30 km (18 miles) above the

A blanket of air covers the Earth's surface

Earth's surface, the *troposphere*. This is where clouds form, rain falls and storms are created, and die.

The atmosphere moves because it is continually redressing a balance. Air flows – the wind blows – from areas of high pressure to areas of low pressure. And the air pressure depends, among other things, on temperature. As air is heated, it expands, it is less dense, it rises and creates an area of low pressure. The sun does not heat the planet evenly; more sunlight reaches the tropics than the poles. The differences in temperature create differences in pressure, and drives the circulating patterns of the winds.

To avoid confusion, when describing the direction of the wind, we always refer to the direction from which it blows, so a northerly wind blows *from* the north, a westerly wind blows from the west, and so on – hence the old saying 'The north wind doth blow, and we shall have snow'.

We have already seen how the air at the equator is heated, and how it creates rainclouds over the oceans. But, although the sun provides the energy to drive the system, it does not heat the air directly in the troposphere; rather, the sunlight heats the ground or the sea, which in turn heats the air. The movement of air in this lower level of the atmosphere is driven by *convection*, the same process that makes a hot-air balloon rise and float.

The system of air masses that rise to create rainforest and sink to create deserts is part of a continuous movement. But the air that has descended over the desert has to go somewhere. Some of it blows back over the surface towards the equator, completing the cycle, but this air does not just blow back from north to south. The crews of the early sailing ships knew that to sail west from Europe, they could first sail south, where they would meet strong, easterly winds that would carry them westwards – reliable, predictable winds that carried them on their journeys of trade and exploration. They named these winds the Trade Winds.

The question then arises – why do the Trade Winds always blow towards the west? In the southern hemisphere, the same phenomenon occurs; the winds blowing towards the equator also blow from east to west. The answer lies in the rotation of the Earth. Imagine a turntable, rotating at a steady speed and then imagine rolling a marble from the centre of the turntable to the edge. It will appear as if the marble follows a curved path. A point on the outside edge of the turntable moves faster than a point nearer the centre, so near the centre the marble is not carried so fast by the turntable as it is at the edge. As the marble moves outwards, it cannot keep up. When it veers to one side, it is because it is lagging behind the movement of the turntable, and it appears to curve away from the direction of rotation.

If we could sit on the turntable and watch the marble from our own viewpoint, we are turning with the turntable, so it will look to us as if the marble is veering off to one side. It seems as if there is a force acting on the marble to make it swerve. This effect is named after the mathematician, Gustave Coriolis, who in 1835 first described how it worked; it is called the Coriolis effect.

On the Earth, then, the winds blowing from the north are not travelling as fast as the Earth at the equator. The Earth rotates from west to east, spinning on its axis, so someone standing on the equator will actually be travelling

faster than someone standing to the north or south. So the Coriolis effect makes the winds veer towards the southwest, rather than directly south, producing the Trade Winds. In the southern hemisphere, the winds blow north towards the equator, and they too are veered towards the west, as they cannot 'keep up' with the movement of the Earth.

Understanding the Coriolis effect is important in understanding much of the Earth's climate, because not only does it affect the movement of the air masses, but it also affects the movement of the ocean currents. Nothing that moves escapes the Coriolis effect; the crew of aircraft flying north–south have to take Coriolis into account when making their navigation calculations.

The Hadley cell, the circulation of air that creates the rainforest and desert, rises at the equator and descends about 1,600 km (1,000 miles) to the north and south, halfway between the equator and the poles, at latitudes of approximately 50°. Only some of this air returns to the equator; the rest is deflected towards the poles. Again, it is veered off by the Coriolis effect, but, this time, the air nearer the equator is moving faster than the ground below it towards the poles. It appears to be ahead of the Earth's rotation and is veered towards the east. So, in the northern hemisphere, a system of warm southwesterly winds blows from the desert belt to the northeast, until it meets the cold polar air of the Arctic. This second circulation is the Ferrel cell, named after William Ferrel, the meteorologist who modified Hadley's theories in the nineteenth century.

The band between the Trade Winds and the southwesterlies, between the Hadley cell and the Ferrel cell, is a band of relative calm. Sailing ships crossing from Europe to the New World could be stranded, becalmed. Precious drinking water was kept for the crew; so, if the ship was carrying livestock, many animals would die. Their carcasses, thrown overboard, gave these dangerous latitudes, about 30° north, their name – the Horse Latitudes.

Earth's surface at equator spinning faster than surface at poles

equator

wind blowing towards pole veers to east (ahead of rotation)

wind blowing towards equator veers to west (lagging behind rotation)

wind blowing towards pole veers to east (ahead of rotation)

The Coriolis effect

High clouds mark the presence of a jet stream

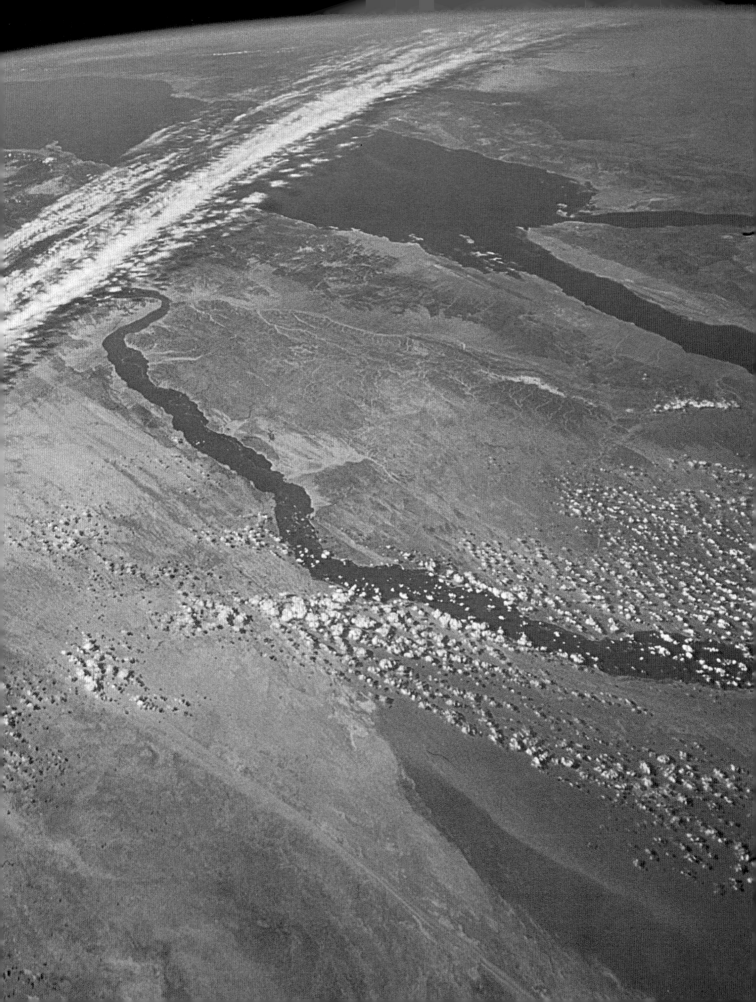

The southwesterlies, moving over the sea, are warm and moist. When this air meets the cold, dry, polar air, the two air masses do not mix easily, so they push against each other. During World War I, a Norwegian research group was studying the development of storms at middle and high latitudes. They likened the boundaries of these air masses to the long lines of soldiers that fought their gruelling battles across battle fronts; the name 'front' came to be used for the interface between the different air masses. These fronts are not stationary; they move as the air masses shift, growing stronger or weaker.

In the Atlantic Ocean, as the air masses clash, they produce huge eddies, great rotating areas of low pressure called *depressions*, and these are responsible for most of the weather that affects Europe. But weather occurs in the bottom layer of the atmosphere, the troposphere, which has a natural 'ceiling', the *tropopause*. In the troposphere – the lower atmosphere – the air is warmer at the surface and gets cooler with height. Warm air at the surface rises, cooling, until either it reaches air of the same density or it meets a barrier. Above this ceiling – the tropopause – the pattern changes, and now the air gets warmer with increasing height as it is exposed to the sun's rays. Warm air rising through the troposphere reaches the bottom of this layer and cannot rise any further. The warm, moist air masses that rise at the equator to create rainforests bump into this natural ceiling, and so have to spread outwards, flowing back to the equator or on to the poles. And above the tropopause clouds do not form. Anyone who has flown in an airliner will have seen how, as they rise above the layers of cloud, there is clear blue sky and sunlight.

But during World War II, when American pilots were trying to reach Japan on their bombing raids, they flew above the tropopause to avoid storms. They found they were being carried by narrow fast bands of winds that blew at up to 320 kph (200 mph). They had found the *jet streams*, high-level winds that encircle the whole planet. In the northern hemisphere, the polar jet stream blows from west to east, and jet aircraft flying from America to Europe can ride this wind, in the same way as the early sailing ships rode the Trade Winds. The jet stream can shorten the journey from the USA to Europe by an hour or so compared to flying in the opposite direction.

The jet streams steer the huge areas of low pressure, the

The devastation left in southern England by the storm of October 1987

depressions, eastwards across the Atlantic towards Europe, bringing high winds and torrential rain, particularly to the west coasts. Reliable weather forecasting is more difficult in say, Britain, than in the USA, because British weather comes from the Atlantic Ocean where there are fewer sources of weather information. Forecasters rely on data from aircraft, shipping, and remote weather buoys, but until the invention of satellite images many of these storms could take the British Isles by surprise.

Even now, storms can be unexpected. It happened in 1987, when a now-infamous storm arrived, unpredicted even by the meteorologists. The unfortunate British weather forecaster, Michael Fish, will be haunted forever by his words on the television forecast of 15 October: 'Earlier on today, apparently a woman rang the BBC and said she'd heard there was a hurricane on the way. Well, if you're watching, don't worry, there isn't...'. He did go on to say: 'But, having said that, actually the weather will become very windy...'.

The meteorologists knew about a large depression to the south, in the Bay of Biscay, and a severe storm with heavy rain and strong winds had been predicted a few days earlier. But late in the evening of 15 October, the depression started to move north. It had been raining heavily all day, and during the night the course of the centre of the storm moved by a hundred miles or so. This took a band of strong winds sweeping across the southeastern counties of England. Winds gusting at more than 160 kph (100 mph) hit without warning, when the sleeping residents could not react or prepare for the onslaught. Fifteen million trees were ripped out of the ground, roofs were blown off buildings, walls were demolished. Overall, 19 people were killed and over £2,000 million worth of damage was done.

The power of the wind need not always be destructive; it can be harnessed to provide energy. Windmills are an

A Picture of the Global Air Masses

The atmosphere is continually in motion over the face of the globe, creating different climates in different parts of the world. There are distinct bands of circulating air that are more or less constant even though the boundaries between them vary, and looking at how they all fit together helps to get an overall picture of our planet's weather patterns.

The energy to drive these bands of air comes from the rotation of the Earth as it spins on its axis, from west to east. The warm air at the equator rises, bumps into the tropopause, and blows away from the equator, creating the Hadley cells; as some of this air blows back to the equator at the surface, it creates the Trade Winds.

At this latitude the air is descending. Over land it creates deserts, but over the sea it creates areas of calm, warm high pressure; these are the Horse Latitudes, where ships could be becalmed.

Descending here, the rest of the air that does not flow to the equator blows towards the poles, creating warm winds. For any air

currents flowing away from the equator, the Coriolis effect makes them veer to the right, so they blow towards the northeast and southeast. These warm southwesterlies and northwesterlies pass over the sea, again picking up moisture, creating Ferrel cells. They meet the cold, dry air from the poles

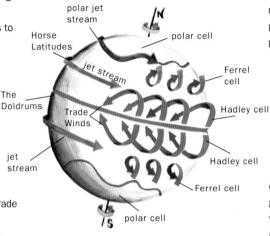

Global air mass circulation

at roughly 60° north and south, and the boundaries where these air masses meet are the polar fronts. In the northern hemisphere, this creates much of the weather that affects North America and Europe.

At the boundaries of these bands of air,

there are high fast winds blowing from west to east. These winds are created by differences in pressure and temperature, and the Earth's rotation – they are called 'jet streams'. The jet stream between the Ferrel cell and the polar air mass is the polar jet stream, and at this boundary the interaction of the warm, moist southwesterlies and the cold, dry polar air creates rotating areas of low pressure, depressions, that are steered towards the east by the jet streams.

The jet streams were predicted by Carl Gustav Rossby, a Swedish meteorologist who worked in the USA. He studied large-scale disturbances in the polar fronts, and found that these boundaries meandered, changing shape, to form huge three-dimensional waves that circulate the globe. These waves are called Rossby waves, and there can be as many as six of them, thousands of kilometres across. As the waves become more extreme, these meanders produce the rotating weather systems we call depressions, and large areas of fixed high pressure, bringing calm, warm weather that can stay around for weeks, called 'blocking highs'.

ancient method of tapping the energy of the wind; originally they were used for turning the huge millstones that were used to grind corn to make flour. The earliest reference to this use of windmills is found in ninth-century Arabic writings which refer to a Persian millwright of AD 644. The concept of windmills was brought to Europe by contact with the Arabs, whereas previously the millstones had been turned by waterwheels. The first windmills appeared in France in 1180 and in England in 1191.

Windmills were also used for pumping water, bringing water up from deep wells, and draining lowland areas. They only went into decline with the invention of steam-driven machinery, in the eighteenth century, although wind pumps were still popular for bringing water out of wells, in rural areas without access to other power. But in the twentieth century, in an increasingly polluted world, wind power provides an alternative to coal or nuclear power stations.

For windmills to generate electrical power, they need to be somewhere where the wind is reliable and constant. In California's Altamont Valley, the morning sun heats the ground which, in turn, warms the air above it. This warm air rises, drawing cold air in from over the sea to replace it. By midday, a strong, constant offshore wind is blowing. A windmill farm, of over 3,000 wind turbines, produces approximately 500,000 megawatt-hours of electricity per year.

So far, though, wind power has yet to be proven; there are not many places in the world that *do* have such a reliable wind source. And, despite the much-publicized discussions on global warming and pollution, many people object to the possibility of huge windmill structures covering their landscape. Wind power, it seems, has yet to be taken seriously as a source of energy.

Wind turbines in the Altamont Valley, California

chapter 8

Rivers in the Sea

The ocean drives planetary chemistry, governs climate and

weather and otherwise provides the cornerstone of the life

support system for all creatures on our planet, from deep

starfish to desert sagebrush. That's why the ocean matters.

If the sea is sick, we'll feel it. If it dies, we die.

Sea Change – *Sylvia Earle*

Looking at Planet Earth from space, it appears that it has the wrong name; a better name would be Planet Water. Over four-fifths of the surface of the planet is covered by ocean, and from a distance it colours the world blue.

The oceans are the final frontier. We know more about the moon than about the depths of the oceans; we have mapped more of the surface of Mars than we have the seabed. The sea is a completely alien world to us. In some places, it is more than 10 km (6 miles) deep; in others it is a matter of metres, but whatever the depth we cannot live naturally under water. Some mammals, like whales and dolphins, adapted to sea life; a sperm whale can hold its breath for an hour, a dolphin 15 minutes, but it is rare for a human to stop breathing – by choice – for more than three minutes. Sea mammals can withstand cold; sea otters have

Riding the currents – a Portuguese Man O'War travels the oceans

dense, thick fur and whales have blubber, allowing them to spend their lives in water close to freezing. Humans are vulnerable to the cold; unless we are relaxing in the shallow, sunlit waters of the tropics, we need the protection of a neoprene wetsuit if we are to spend any time in the sea.

This means that the ocean is the ultimate mystery to us. We can use telescopes to see into space, but to see into the darkness of the ocean takes equipment as least as sophisticated as the space shuttle. Less than 1 per cent of the ocean floor is mapped in detail, and the number of people who have visited these depths – and returned – can be numbered in hundreds.

The obvious difference between the oceans and the other water on the planet – rain, streams, rivers and lakes – is that seawater is salty. Roughly 3 per cent of seawater consists of dissolved salts, which makes the water undrinkable. So where does the salt come from? Most of the salts consist of sodium and chlorine in solution, and when sea-

water evaporates it leaves behind sodium chloride, familiar to us as sea salt. There are traces of other elements in seawater, but they are negligible in comparison to the salt.

The water in the oceans is part of the great cycle of water on the planet. It arrives in the ocean by rainfall, and from the rivers and streams; it leaves the oceans by evaporation, to form clouds, rain, and fall back into the ocean again. As the fresh water in streams runs over rocks, it dissolves different salts from these rocks. The cumulative effect of streams and rivers adds much of the salts to the sea. But this is not the only source. Volcanic eruptions continually bring materials from deep inside the Earth; venting gases bring carbon dioxide, chlorides, sulphates, all of which eventually make their way to the oceans. But

Cold, salty water at the poles sinks to create slow-moving deep ocean currents

when water leaves the sea it does so by evaporation, and so leaves the minerals behind.

Salts are added to the ocean from these different sources, but if this were the only process the seas would have been getting more and more salty over time, and this does not seem to be happening. So where is the salt going? Animals and plants that live in the ocean use minerals to build their shells, so silicon, calcium, phosphorus are used up from the seawater. Clay particles brought into the sea by rivers absorb potassium and sodium and remove them as they settle. A combination of these processes, and others, means that the amount of salt in the ocean stays roughly constant.

The saltiness – or salinity – of seawater is slightly different in different places across the globe, and it is these differences that contribute to the slow movement of deep-water currents. Areas of the ocean where there is a lot of rain are less salty than areas where there is little rain, and more water evaporates than is added. Whereas on land

A coconut palm, washed up by the ocean currents, germinates on solid ground

there are areas of rainforest and desert, in the oceans there are equivalent areas of salty and less salty water. There are differences in temperature as well as salinity; the warmest water is generally in a belt round the globe where there is most sunlight. This belt moves south of the equator when it is winter in the northern hemisphere, and moves north again in the summer.

The more salty water is, the heavier it is, so salty water tends to sink. The same applies to cold water – the colder it is, the heavier it is. So there are different layers in the oceans, depending on the temperature and salinity.

The coldest, most salty water sinks to the bottom of the ocean; this happens at the Arctic and Antarctic regions. In the north Atlantic, around the Arctic icecap, the cold, salty water sinks and spreads southwards, forming the North Atlantic Deep Water mass. When it eventually reaches the south Atlantic, it joins the deepest, coldest water that circulates round the Antarctic continent, the Antarctic Bottom Water. These very deep, very slow-moving currents do not seem to have a direct relevance to us, but it is these huge masses of water that transport heat round the planet. They take hundreds of years to complete their circulation, but eventually this water mixes with the warmer water above it, rising to the surface. It then flows back to the polar areas where it sinks once more, completing the cycle.

The actual circulations are far more complex than this, but not only are deep currents a major influence on the world's climate, they are crucial to marine life. Deep water tends to be very rich, carrying nutrients. As everything in the sea dies, from microscopic plankton to massive whales, the remains sink to the bottom, breaking down, decomposing. Rather like the soil in a forest, this deep, fertile water provides nutrition for other creatures; when it comes to the surface, it supports rich communities of marine life.

As well as a very slow circulation of water between the

deep and the surface, the oceans are continually circulating in the ocean basins, in *gyres* – surface currents that are pushed by the prevailing winds and affected by the Earth's rotation. The water in the oceans is not flat and stable; it sloshes around, like water in a bucket. Like the winds, the oceans are affected by the Coriolis force; this makes the gyres in the northern hemisphere – the north Atlantic and the north Pacific – rotate in a clockwise direction, while the gyres in the southern hemisphere rotate in an anticlockwise direction.

The rotation of the Earth, from west to east, causes the water of the oceans to 'pile up' on the west side of the ocean basins. In the north Atlantic, this effect, together with the effect of the Trade Winds, makes the water pile up against the east coast of North America. The sea level is slightly higher on the west side of the ocean than on the east.

The gyre in the north Atlantic flows northwards up the east coast of America, across the north Atlantic and southwards down the east coast of west Africa. It creates what is perhaps the most famous of the great ocean currents, the Gulf Stream. This mighty river in the sea flows from the warm Gulf of Mexico northeast past the coast of North America, carrying warm water across the north Atlantic,

---

The Wide Sargasso Sea

To the western side of the Atlantic Ocean, in the vicinity of Bermuda, is a still, strange sea – the Sargasso Sea. It is a slow, revolving layer of warm water, a kilometre (half a mile) deep, that floats on the colder water underneath, 'trapped' in the circulating gyre of the north Atlantic. It is a warm, calm area with little rain; evaporation makes the water slightly more salty than average. Its gentle clockwise rotation gives the sea an oval shape, almost two-thirds the area of the continental USA; it is bound to the west and north by the Gulf Stream, to the east by the North Atlantic current and to the south by the North Equatorial current.

It was first noticed by Columbus on his famous voyage in 1492. His ships came across an area thick with a form of seaweed, and they could see fish and crabs in its depths that would normally be found in coastal waters. They thought they were close to land, but they were still 1,000 km (620 miles) offshore.

The weed they could see was *sargassum*, a form of seaweed that floats freely in the ocean, held up by hollow floats that look like little grapes. Because of the sharp, leaf-like shape of the weed, it is sometimes called *sea holly*. Huge rafts of sargassum stretch in a tangle from horizon to horizon, and crews of early sailing ships were unduly concerned they would get caught up in it, unable to escape. The sargassum never touches land, and reproduces while still afloat; pieces break off and grow into new patches of

A sargassum toadfish hides among the seaweed

weed. The currents that flow around the Sargasso Sea contain the seaweed in the circular area.

The warm, clear water is not very fertile, and there is very little mixing with the cold water further down. But the sargassum offers shelter in the open ocean, so the rafts of seaweed carry a self contained ecosystem as they slowly drift round and round in the Atlantic.,

Two types of creatures can be found here. The residents, like the sargassum crabs, the toadfish, the sargassum fish, live all their lives within the rafts, and have evolved a colour scheme that makes them indistinguishable from the seaweed.

The visitors, small, young fish, come to the rafts for shelter, for protection from the predators of the open ocean. Unfortunately, the predators often come to the sargassum rafts for that very reason; big ocean-dwelling fish, such as dolphinfish, are attracted by these young fish lurking in the depths of the weeds.

As this huge layer of water is rotating, it does not escape the Coriolis effect. This causes the water to 'pile up' in the centre, forming a dome, and in the middle of the Sargasso sea the level is 1 m (3 ft) or so higher than the outside.

bringing a mild, although wet, climate to western Europe. The water can be as warm as 25°C (77°F), sweeping round the southern tip of Florida. The 'piling up' of the water in the Atlantic channels the Gulf Stream into a river 80 km (50 miles) or so wide as it passes Florida at 6.5 kph (4 mph), but when it reaches New York it has spread out to 500 km (300 miles) wide and has slowed down. By the time it moves northeast across the Atlantic, it is travelling at 8 km (5 miles) a day, and is now officially called the North Atlantic Drift. It has split into several streams, one of which, the central flow, reaches the coast of Europe. Early explorers soon learned that if they hitched a ride on the current, they would save two weeks on the return journey from the Americas to Europe. One of the first recorded observations of the Gulf Stream was from the crew of the *Matthew*, the ship that took John Cabot on his voyages of exploration to North America in 1497. His crew kept their beer in the bottom of the hold to keep it cool, but while crossing the Atlantic they found, to their dismay, that the beer had turned sour. Without realizing it, they had sailed into warm water, crossing into the Gulf Stream.

The most westerly tip of Europe is southwest Ireland, and the Gulf Stream brushes the coast of County Kerry. This sweep of warm water keeps Kerry free from frost and snow, creating conditions unique to this part of northern Europe. Ancient oak forests stay warm and damp, so that everything is covered in a vibrant green moss, making the woodlands resemble a scene from Tolkien's stories. And within just a few square kilometres, lives a creature that is here simply because of the effect of the Gulf Stream. The Kerry spotted slug.

The Kerry spotted slug is, as its name suggests, a small, pretty, green, grey and white dappled slug. It is only found here and in one other place – the warm, damp forests of Portugal. It lives on boulders and trees, under the moss,

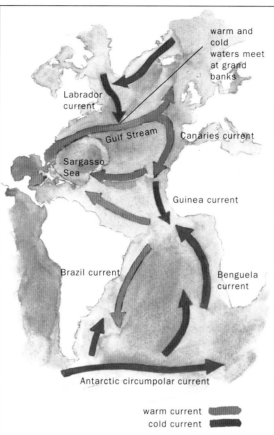

Currents in the Atlantic Ocean

and when disturbed curls up into a ball. It is not known for sure whether the slug was found all over Europe until the last ice age made everywhere else too cold for it, or whether it was somehow brought to Ireland from the Mediterranean. Either way, it thrives in Kerry in the mild, damp conditions brought by the warm water, much warmer than other places as far north.

As the Gulf Stream sweeps up the coast of North America it meets a cold current flowing south from the Arctic, the Labrador current. As some of the warm water from the Gulf Stream mixes with this cold water at the Grand Banks, off the coast of Newfoundland, it swirls and churns up sediments that are rich in nutrients. This creates very fertile water, so much so that this area once supported the most productive fisheries in the world. Capelin thrive here, and in turn they provided food for enormous numbers of cod. The huge populations of fish in turn support colonies of thousands of seabirds – gannets, guillemots and razorbills nest on the cliffs. For centuries, fishermen came here to help themselves to the harvest of fish, even making the dangerous crossing of the Atlantic from Europe to cash in on the bonanza centuries before Columbus discovered the New World. But this was such a lucrative trade that the fishermen who came here kept these fisheries a closely guarded secret.

In the northern hemisphere, in the great circulating gyres, the warm water flows northwards up the west side of the ocean basin, is cooled at the Arctic, and flows as a cold current down the east side of the ocean. The Pacific Ocean has the warm Kuroshio current which corresponds to the Gulf Stream in the Atlantic. And, as the waters of the Kuroshio current are cooled in the Arctic, they flow south becoming the California current down the California coast.

Overleaf: **Kelp forests teem with life in the Pacific coastal waters of California**

This water churns up nutrients from the seabed, and is so fertile it creates the massive kelp forests that support a kaleidoscope of life. Ribbons of kelp grow from the seabed to the surface, sometimes as long as 120 m (400 ft); the kelp offers shelter, hiding-places for fish within its ribbons.

On the surface of the kelp forests, sea otters spend much of their lives floating on their backs or playing in the surf. They survive in the cold water because their fur is so thick; the water never makes direct contact with their skin. It is the thickest fur of any mammal, providing both water-proofing and insulation. It is to the sea otters' advantage to live in the cold water here, as they feed on shellfish that thrive on the seabed. They dive down to bring shellfish, such as abalone, to the surface; and sea otters are among the few mammals other than us to use tools. To break the shell, the sea otter holds it on its chest as it floats on its back, and bangs a rock against the shell to break it.

The habitats along the coasts of the continents are cre-

Clubmoss drapes the trees of the temperate rainforest of the north-west coast of America

ated by the currents and the shape of the landscape. Further north than California, along the coast of Oregon and Washington state, and extending into Canada's British Columbia, the coast is cloaked in rainforest. This is not the hot, steaming, tropical rainforest found around the equatorial belt, but cool, temperate rainforest. But, as in the tropics, it is created by immense amounts of rain. In the Pacific Ocean, the warm Kuroshio current, like the Gulf Stream in the Atlantic, sweeps across the north towards the northwest coast of the north American continent. And, again, as in the tropics, the air over this current picks up moisture, but here, it is blown against the mountains that rise almost sheer out of the coast. On the Olympic peninsula, between Puget Sound and the ocean, the Olympic mountains force this warm, wet air upwards, so that it drops its rain, as much as 3,800 mm (150 in) a year, creating rainforest.

The warm current to the west keeps the area free from frost and snow, and to the east the great mountain chain of the Rockies shelters the area from the bitterly cold winters of the interior of the continent. A mixture of Sitka spruce and bigleaf maple grow near the coast, and further inland western hemlock and red cedar form the canopy. The forest floor is covered with ferns, and everywhere is the sound of water. Mist forms over the forest as water evaporates from the leaves, and everything glistens, shimmering in every conceivable shade of green.

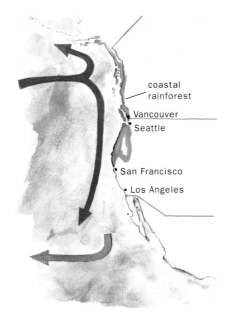

coastal rainforest
Vancouver
Seattle
San Francisco
Los Angeles

The great circulating currents of the oceans create conditions on the land they pass, influencing the climate and hence the life that lives there. If any of these currents were to change direction or weaken, not only would the marine life be affected, but the habitats they create would also be drastically altered. The conveyor belt of the oceans, transporting heat around the globe, has such a powerful effect on the climate that it dictates where and how life can flourish on Planet Water.

Currents in the northeast Pacific Ocean

Dr Sylvia Earle

Sylvia Earle is an oceanographer, a marine scientist who works with the organization Deep Ocean Exploration and Research.

It's amazing how little we actually know about the deep sea. Fewer than two dozen of the hot vent areas have been explored. And think of how big the ocean is. I think less than one-tenth of 1 per cent of the deep sea has been explored at all.

I worry a lot about what's happening to the oceans, about what we're putting into the sea, through the changing chemistry of the oceans, through the combination of hard trash and sewage and other chemicals that we have put into the oceans in recent times. I worry a lot about overfishing, about what we're removing wholesale from the oceans. Not just individual species, as in the days of whaling, but now nets that actually take whole ecosystems in single bites, as they crisscross the ocean floor. Some nets are so large they would consume a dozen jet aircraft in one bite.

Presently, the oceans of the world are in trouble; most people simply aren't aware of it. There's the perception that the oceans are so big and so vast that human beings cannot do very much to harm them. But in my lifetime the oceans have changed signifi-

cantly, partly because of what we're putting in, partly because of what we're taking out.

Our life depends on the nature of the oceans. It isn't just what we take out of it to eat, and what gets incorporated into our systems because of what has gone into the fish, the lobsters, the clams and the oysters, that concentrates some of the material that we put into the sea – although that certainly ought to be cause for concern. When you think of the Earth as a whole, this is an ocean planet. Life on Earth depends on the existence of this great big ocean system.

The ocean's not only a home to most of life on Earth – more than 90 per cent of the biosphere is ocean. But more than that, it drives climate and weather. It's a great

thermal regulator. In spite of what seems like really high temperatures in the summer and low temperatures in the winter, all of this is within a range that we human beings can tolerate. We couldn't live on Mars in the same way that we live here. If we do succeed in lofting ourselves to some distant planet in space, it would be because we take our life support system with us. The oxygen, the water, the ability to create an atmosphere, and food. We take it all for granted. It derives from the fact there is an ocean here, that makes this planet hospitable for us. If the ocean is in trouble, so are we.

Sylvia Earle is passionate about the need to treat the oceans with respect

chapter 9 Hawaii

Red-eyed Pele!

Woman with eyes like the noni-dyed kapa!

Woman who sends rain on the lowlands –

Black rain of rocks and hot lava!

Hawaiian Antiquities and Folklore – Abraham Fornander

There are two sisters – neighbours – who live alongside each other in a snarling truce. They cannot live apart, they cannot live together. Their battleground is the island chain of Hawaii.

One sister is Namaka o Kahai, the goddess of the sea. The other is Pele, goddess of fire. As Pele was growing up, she lived with her family on the island of Far Kahiki, but, before long, she wanted to leave, to see the world. Her brother, Kamoho-alii, the shark god, built her a canoe, and, with some of her brothers and sisters, she travelled across the sea. Eventually, she arrived at the island of Nihau, a small island at the very north of the Hawaiian chain; here, she dug into the ground with her sacred spade, her *paoa*, and brought land out of the earth to make a new home.

But Pele and Namaka were rivals in love. They fought bitterly over a handsome young chief, and Namaka, the sea, in a fit of jealousy, destroyed Pele's home. Pele moved to the next island, Kuai'i, where again she plunged the *paoa* into the ground and brought up lava, creating the hill now called Pu'u o Pele, the 'Hill of Pele'. But Namaka could not

Fire meets water – volcanic lava reaches the sea on Hawaii's Big Island

forgive her, and, again, she caught up with her sister, driving her out of this home.

Pele fled to Oahu, where she created a fire pit as before, but Namaka caused salt water to rise up and drown it; it is now known as Salt Lake. Still on Oahu, Pele dug a fire crater at Diamond Head, but it seemed she could not win. The sea quenched the fire and Pele escaped to Maui. By now, the quarrel was so vitriolic that Namaka caught up with her and they fought; Pele's body was broken, her bones smashed and left at Kaiwi o Pele (the 'Bones of Pele'). Namaka had won, and she left Pele for dead.

But a goddess has magical powers, and Pele came back to life, stronger than before. She made her way to the island of Hawaii, the 'Big Island', and, using her *paoa*, made her biggest home yet, a lovenest to share with her handsome chief. She still lives deep in the crater of Kilauea, and is a lady with a reputation for a fiery temper. She stamps her foot and creates earthquakes, she gets angry and sends out the lava flows. Sometimes she appears to humans, usually before an eruption; it may be as a beautiful young maiden, it may be as an old hag. However she appears, it is always wise to treat her well, and treat her home, the volcano, with a healthy respect.

The chain of islands, known by the name of its largest, Hawaii, is the most remote in the world. The islands are marketed as 'paradise' and are the holiday destination for six million tourists a year; sun, surf, stunningly beautiful beaches and spectacular scenery offer escapism to all. Over half the tourists that head for Hawaii make their way to Waikiki, on the east side of Honolulu on the island of Oahu. Waikiki Beach is the gathering place for the beautiful people, and Honolulu itself a city built on the combined wealth of America and Japan. It has modern skyscrapers, shops that cater for the trinket market for tourists as well as the expensive tastes of the wealthy, and to the west of Honolulu is Pearl Harbor, the US Navy base.

Four thousand km (2,500 miles) from anywhere, in the middle of the Pacific Ocean, these islands are among the youngest land on the planet. They were created by volcanoes, and on Hawaii the act of creation is still happening. These islands are at most five million years old and Hawaii, the youngest, only half a million years old. On the geological scale of things, this makes Hawaii something of an upstart.

A glance at the map of the active volcanic regions of the world, where the great continental plates crash into each other or split apart shows that Hawaii is nowhere near one of these regions. So why, in the middle of a stable oceanic plate, is it so active?

The hot spot is an isolated plume of plastic rock, welling up from deep inside the earth, possibly even as deep as the core itself. As it rises, it melts the surrounding rock, creating magma, and erupts in the middle of the ocean. The Pacific plate moves over this hot spot at a rate of roughly 7.5 cm (3 in) a year, heading northwest. The Pacific plate is the one that slides alongside the North American plate at the San Andreas fault, causing earthquakes in California; eventually, this plate reaches the Aleutian trench where it sinks into the Earth, in the process known as subduction. Each volcano is formed over the hot spot, then drifts away, becoming quiet once more.

The largest of the islands, Hawaii, is still active today. Two mountains, Mauna Loa and Mauna Kea, form the island itself. Again, the most activity occurs on the southeast

Nihau
Kuai'i
Oahu
Honolulu
Molakai
Lanai
Maui
Kahoolawe
Mauna Loa
Maune Kea
Kilauea crater
Hawaii ('Big Island')
Hilo
Loihi
lava flow to sea

0   miles   200

The Hawaiian island chain

of the island as it moves over the hot spot. Mauna Kea, the 'white mountain', is silent, dormant now, and is the highest mountain on the planet measured from the seabed. It rises over 9 km (5½ miles) directly from ocean floor to summit, and although the climate is pleasantly tropical at sea level, there is often snow on the top of Mauna Kea.

Mauna Loa, the 'long mountain', is almost as high, and both mountains are deceptive. They are both shield volcanoes, formed by gentle, slow lava flow, creating smooth, shallow domes. Looking at them from a distance, they look easily accessible; there is no perspective that gives a sense of sheer, dramatic size, nothing to give a clue to their 4,000 m (13,000 ft) height. A single road climbs up to the observatory near the summit, a long, winding track that seems to go on for ever through the broken lava as far as the eye can see.

The central crater of Mauna Loa itself is silent, but on its southeast flank the active crater of Kilauea still pours lava into the sea. Kilauea is Pele's current home. Around the crater, the air smells of sulphur from the fumarole vents, and white tropicbirds swoop and dive around the inside of the crater. The fascination of this place draws visitors from all over the world, and the area is now a National Park. The fire pit, Halemaumau, inside the Kilauea caldera, was molten as recently as the nineteenth century. In 1872, Mark Twain described his visit to Halemaumau at night:

The greater part of the vast floor of the desert under us was black as ink and apparently smooth and level; but over a square mile of it was ringed and streaked with a thousand branching streams of liquid and gorgeously brilliant fire! It looked like a colossal railroad map of the State of Massachusetts done in chain lightning against a midnight sky. Imagine it – imagine a coal black sky shivered into a tangled network of angry fire! Here and there were gleaming holes twenty feet in diameter, broken in the dark crust, and in them the melted lava – the colour a dazzling white just tinged with yellow – was boiling and surging furiously.

Satellite view of the Hawaiian islands looking south

For a visitor today, Halemaumau has cooled enough to have a solid crust, and its activity is only hinted at by the fumaroles. But underneath there is a chamber of molten lava, and this lava finds its way down the side of Mauna Loa via underground lava tubes. At the coast, it emerges as a slow-moving, sticky flow that slides into the sea, creating billowing clouds of hydrochloric acid that can be seen for miles. As dusk falls, visitors come to the edge of an earlier, cooled lava flow to watch the red glow from the lava light up the night sky. At regular intervals of a few years, the flow of lava changes direction and claims a new patch of coast. The road that once ran round the 'Big Island' now disappears under the cooled lava flow. Park Rangers monitor the lava activity and courteously dissuade enthusiastic tourists from approaching the flow too closely. Pele is creating real estate; the 'Big Island' is expanding into the ocean.

Living with Pele

Hawaii's volcanoes are, by geological standards, fairly gentle and predictable. Their shape has given their name to all volcanoes of this type; they are *shield volcanoes*. Their regular, shallow-sloping sides have been built up from layer upon layer of runny lava that spills down the slopes.

Whether a volcano will be gentle like those of Hawaii, or dramatic and dangerous, erupting in a violent explosion, depends on the way the magma is formed deep underground. The magma that creates Hawaii's volcanoes escapes steadily; the pressure rarely builds up enough to cause a major explosion. It may spray into the air as a fountain, or it may just spill over, running down the slope to the sea.

Kilauea is a volcano that allows people to approach, if they do not take it for granted. Scientists study the lava flows, taking samples and monitoring the activity of the eruptions. Film-makers and photographers capture the beauty and power of the volcano. John Kjargaard, a photographer, lives in Hawaii and specializes in filming volcanoes in Hawaii, New Zealand and Russia. However friendly Kilauea may seem when he is out filming, he treats it with respect.

I get scared all the time; I think if you're out there and you don't get scared, you should be in another business. You really stay in touch with everything that's going on around you out there, but there are always things where you are caught by surprise.

If you want to get good footage, you've got to be in the right place at the right time. What you don't want to be is in the wrong place at the wrong time, and you can easily go from being in the right place to being in the wrong place in only a few seconds or a few feet. The wind may shift and you end up in a gas cloud; you may be close to a fountain which you're shooting and again the wind changes, and you find yourself under a cloud of tephra or Pele's hair, or just tremendous heat. A blast of wind may come from some place you haven't calculated and the air temperature could go from normal, say 100°, up to 500° in seconds.

He relies on experience to keep himself out of danger.

Almost everything that occurs out there is preceded by a sound, and you must be able to hear this sound and recognize that it's different from all the other roars and rumbles and rushes, so you stop. If you can't figure out what that sound is, you get out of there immediately.

The local people are used to living with Pele's moods. Kjargaard again:

In Hawaii, where you have volcanoes around you all the time, you just accept that they are there and you accept that if you live down slope of an active volcano you may have your house overrun by lava.

I think it's a fairly strong belief among Hawaiians of Pele being the Goddess of Fire. I see Pele as Mother Nature so when I'm out on lava flows I don't do things like throw my trash in the flow, though some people do. I respect nature and, to me, Pele is the deity I see when I see nature.

Offerings left to Pele at the edge of Kilauea crater

The rope-like texture of *pahoehoe* lava

Volcanic activity at Hawaii creates two distinctive types of lava, and these have now given their names to lava classisification the world over. *Pahoehoe* ('pah-hoy-hoy') is the hot, runny, slow-moving lava that, when it cools, does so with a ropy, folded effect like thick batter. It moves steadily, and could be outrun by a reasonably fit adult, and the cooled surface is smooth, often reflecting the sun like pewter. *Aa* ('ah-ah') is broken and chunky, caused by the cooling lava tumbling over itself as it moves. Once cool, its rough, jagged, black surface contains shards of volcanic glass; to walk on *aa* is a hazard in itself. The rock is fragile, with hidden, deceptive holes, and a slip can mean cuts, as well as bruises, from the glass. Usually, *aa* moves more slowly than *pahoehoe* but is less predictable; it can suddenly lurch forward without warning.

Both forms of lava cool to give the rock known as basalt, and erosion of basalt produces another bizarre feature of the landscape in Hawaii. On the older islands, and the windward sides, the beaches are made of crushed coral, giving the brilliant white sand that contrasts with blue water to the delight of the tourist industry. But on 'Big Island', where the waves break down the basalt from Kilauea's flow, they form beaches of jet-black sand, a stark contrast to the white foam of the surf.

The area around Halemaumau is still considered sacred to Pele, and offerings are still made to her at the edge of the crater. Flowers, incense sticks, food and alcohol are presented to her and left on the ground, where they remain untouched by visitors as a mark of respect.

Hawaii has extremes of climate; from the snow to sun-soaked beaches, from sumptuous rainforests to parched desert. Some of this discrepancy is due to altitude which ranges from sea level to 4,000 m (13,000 ft), but the variation in rainfall is due to Hawaii's geographical position in the middle of the Pacific Ocean. The islands are in the path of the Trade Winds, which blow from the northeast, and as they do so they collect moisture. But, as they reach Hawaii, these saturated winds are forced upwards and drop their rain on the northeast, windward sides of the islands. The result is a chain of islands with lush rainforest on one side and parched desert on the other, leeward side.

But the rainforest supports a bizarre variety of life – bizarre because most of the wildlife on Hawaii arrived by accident some thousands of years ago, on the wind or on the ocean currents. But once on dry land the journey was over. Evolution had a field day. Around the craters of Kilauea, the native Hawaiian goose, the *ne-ne* ('nay-nay'),

The Hawaiian goose, the *ne-ne*, lives around the crater of the volcano

feeds and nests in the *kipukas*, or isolated patches of forest missed by the lava flow. These descended from Canada geese that lost their way on migration, and the population is unique to Hawaii. They were dangerously close to extinction in the early part of this century, but a breeding programme in England's Wildfowl Trust, and in Hawaii, is restoring their numbers.

The island of Kuai'i, the northwesternmost main island, bears the brunt of the Trade Winds, and receives so much rain that it is the wettest place on Earth. The rain falling on the windward side of the islands not only creates lush rainforest, but waterfalls also carve their way into the landscape. This produces knife-edge cliffs and deep gorges. Kuai'i boasts its own 'Grand Canyon', Waimea Canyon, a glorious, layered gorge, continually changing colour as the clouds pass over. As one of Pele's original homes, Kuai'i has been returned to Namaka. Water dominates this landscape as fire dominates the Big Island.

Further north again, the sea has claimed the islands back for itself. Midway Island, once as high and dramatic as Kuai'i, is now flat, eroded by wind and waves. Formerly a US Air Force Base, it is now a wildlife sanctuary for colonies of albatross. Soon, it will return to the ocean, as have all the islands to the north, now under the waves. The

Long, Tall Island

A distance of 40 km (25 miles) to the southeast of Hawaii's 'Big Island', Pele is building her new home. Named 'Loihi', meaning 'long, tall one', this island measures 13 km by 26 km (8 miles by 16 miles) and rises 4 km (2½ miles) above the seabed. Loihi is an active volcano, going through its birth pangs, under 1,000 m (3,300 ft) of water.

So how do we know what is happening down there? There is nothing to see on the surface. But when the seabed was mapped with sonar several decades ago, the underwater mound was discovered. Then, in the 1980s, scientists realized that this was not just an undersea mountain, it was an active volcano; they began to study it, using a submersible to take photographs and collect rock samples. They left sensors on the seabed to record vibrations and changes in pressure, and collected them weeks or months later to retrieve the data.

Loihi was definitely active; swarms of earthquakes showed that magma was moving around in the depths of the volcano. And on the summit, in a large area roughly the area of a football field, hydrothermal vents belched out water at boiling point; they were named 'Pele's vents'. Visibility is poor; when the submersible crew look out, the dust and ash in the murky water stops them seeing more than a few metres. But for several years Loihi was fairly quiet, a gentle volcano, keeping itself to itself.

Then, in July 1996, the activity increased; over a six-hour period there were 40 quakes measured. It was obvious something violent was happening. Within days, scientists were above the site in their research ship, the *Ka'imikai O Kanaloa* (Hawaiian for 'searcher god of the sea'), using sonar to map the area below. At first they thought the equipment might be malfunctioning; something was not where it should be. The familiar summit of Loihi, the area of Pele's Vents, had disappeared, and in its place there was a huge, gaping hole. The peak of the mountain had collapsed into a crater, 600 m (2,000 ft) across and 240 m (800 ft) deep; this crater was renamed Pele's Pit.

When the earthquakes subsided and calm returned to the area, the scientists went down in their submersible, *Pisces V*. Visibility was low, but they could see that the whole area was a wreck; new boulders were strewn across the seabed, the volcano completely rearranged. But although Pele's Vents had gone there were new hydrothermal vents, and within a matter of weeks they had been colonized by bacteria, living off the minerals carried by the erupting seawater.

Loihi is still growing, still surprising the scientists that monitor it. To keep a constant watch on the volcano, a remote, unmanned observatory is being prepared to be positioned permanently on site, deep underwater. The Hawaii Underwater Geo-Observatory (HUGO) will be connected to the main island via a fibre-optic cable; it will mean that any changes will be monitored as they happen, by the sensors placed around the volcano; a seismometer will register tremors, a microphone will listen for sounds and a pressure transducer will identify any changes in depth, which could happen if the summit of the volcano inflates or drops due to magma movement.

And despite all our efforts to follow Loihi's progress none of us will be here to witness the new island breaking the surface; at the current rate of change, Loihi will appear as the latest addition to the Hawaiian chain, Pele's new home, in about 10,000 years time.

Formation of Hawaii's new island, Loihi, off the coast of 'Big Island'

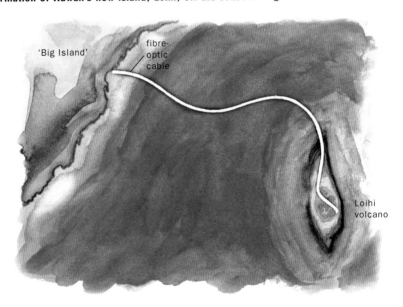

first of the islands to be formed by this hot spot is now about to be subducted into the Aleutian Trench; these islands are part of the Emperor Chain, all part of the same arc as Hawaii.

But Pele is building a new home for herself. Fifty km (30 miles) to the southeast of 'Big Island', a new volcano is emerging under the waves. Still below sea level, Loihi is now 5,000 m (16,500 ft) above the sea floor and rising. At the rate it is growing now, Loihi will appear above the surface in 10,000 years or so, but it is possible that, if Pele loses her temper, becomes more active, then this could happen within a few centuries. Pele, the destroyer, is also the creator. A new island will join the Hawaiian chain, and Pele will have won another battle against her sister, the sea.

chapter 10

The Big Winds

...the annual loss of life, occasioned by the wreck or foundering

of British vessels at sea, may, on the same grounds (i.e. 'the

boisterous nature of the weather and the badness of the ships'),

be fairly estimated at not less than One Thousand persons in

each year...

Report from the Parliament Select Committee

appointed to inquire into the cause of shipwrecks, 1839

The Earth is a planet of two halves. All the activity of the winds and oceans in the northern hemisphere is reflected – roughly – in the southern hemisphere. There *are* differences, owing to several factors, not least the different amounts of landmasses; the northern hemisphere has more than twice as much land as the southern. Ocean currents have different effects as they pass around different landmasses.

In both hemispheres the Trade Winds that blow towards the equator, blow from the east. They meet at a band that runs along the equator, roughly 3–7° of latitude to the north and south. They meet and combine high above the surface of the ocean, but at the surface the air is still. Scientists call this band by the catchy name of the Inter-tropical Convergence Zone (ITCZ), but to the intrepid crews of the first sailing ships it had a different name, one that struck terror into the hardiest mariners. The Doldrums.

Caribbean tranquillity – the calm before the storm

To cross from the northern to the southern hemisphere, sailing ships had to cross the equator, and take the risk of being trapped in the Doldrums. If they were, the result was a living nightmare. At the hottest part of the tropical ocean, the wind could die, leaving a sailing ship helpless and immobile. This might last for weeks, in the humid, sweltering heat. Supplies would run out, and gradually food would be used up, but – most importantly – the crew could find themselves with no drinking water. The most famous survivor of the Doldrums is surely Coleridge's 'Ancient Mariner', who, like many other sailors who were becalmed, lost his mind.

The only hope for a ship marooned in this way was to drift with the ocean currents until, with luck, it could catch up with the Trade Winds again. And to make the crossing of the equator even more difficult, the ITCZ – the Doldrums – moves north and south with the seasons, so its exact position and extent was unpredictable.

But, although the Doldrums strike terror into the crews

of sailing ships, they play a crucial role in the planet's weather systems; it is here that monsters are born. In the Atlantic Ocean, north of the equator, weather disturbances such as low pressure in the upper part of the atmosphere track westwards from west Africa. If they disturb the warm, moist air in the Doldrums, the air becomes unstable, and a pocket of warm air starts to rise. This creates an area of low pressure, but as air begins to flow inwards to replace the rising air, the Earth's Coriolis effect turns this air flow – a *tropical depression* – into a rotating system.

In the northern hemisphere, these winds blow anticlockwise around the area of low pressure. To see what happens to the wind speed, we can imagine what happens to an ice-skater, spinning on the ice. With her arms stretched out, she spins at a certain speed, but, as she brings her arms in towards her body, she spins faster and faster. This is an important principle called *conservation of angular momentum*. Within the tropical depression, this means that the nearer the winds are to the centre, the stronger they are; as the depression forms over warm tropical seas, the winds evaporate more water, transferring energy from the ocean to the depression.

The rotating winds create spiralling bands of cloud and violent updrafts. Sudden, rising columns of moist air generate thunderstorms, and torrential rain feeds even more energy into the system. As long as the sustained wind speeds are less than 61 kph (38 mph), this is still a tropical depression, but if the winds increase beyond this it becomes a *tropical storm.*

When a tropical storm makes landfall, the damage comes from high winds, torrential rain and possible flooding. Some regions bear the brunt of these storms; in the Atlantic Ocean, Central America and the Caribbean islands are battered by tropical storms between June and November. The native people lived with the threat of violence and destruction; to them the storm was an entity, a god or goddess. For the Maya of Central America, the storm was a vengeful god, Hurakan. When the Spanish conquistadors arrived in the sixteenth century, they named the most powerful of these storms after the Mayan god – the hurricane.

A tropical storm earns the name 'hurricane' when sustained wind speeds are more than 120 kph (74 mph). A hurricane is the most powerful, violent storm on the planet; in a single day, it can release 8,000 times more than the

The eye of the hurricane in the centre of the swirling banks of cloud

electrical power generated in a day in the whole of the USA. This is equivalent to 500,000 Nagasaki-type 20-kiloton bombs exploding in one day. For a tropical storm to become such a powerful entity, there must be certain conditions. The warm sea holds a lot of heat, but, for there to be enough water to sustain this energy, a hurricane initially forms over deep water; there is not enough energy in shallow water less than 60 m (200 ft) or so deep. And there must be little wind shear; in other words, the winds do not vary much with height. If this was the case, the variation in winds with height would dissipate the storm's energy and the hurricane would not form.

When these conditions *are* fulfilled, and the hurricane forms, it can be as much as 500 km (300 miles) across. This storm moves over the sea, in a curved path, at speeds up to 80 kph (50 mph). As it does, the low pressure creates a dome of water; over the sea, this is hardly noticeable, but as the hurricane approaches land and this surge is forced into shallow water, it creates a *storm surge*, a wall of water as high as 4.5 m (15 ft), bringing sudden, violent flooding to coastal areas. A storm surge can create as much damage as the high winds, and the flooding from the torrential rain.

Hurricanes are measured in categories depending on the sustained wind speed; the mildest, a category 1, has winds of 120 kph (75 mph), whereas the strongest, a category 5, has winds in excess of 250 kph (155 mph).

With the invention of satellite communication, we can now watch these storms forming and make some estimate of where they are heading, and how fast. But before modern technology, a hurricane gave little warning of its arrival; in 1900, 8,000 people died as a hurricane devastated Galveston, Texas. There was no time to evacuate. Yet, in some areas, native people could read the subtle clues in the natural world about them. The behaviour of birds or animals could give a warning that a storm was on its way. Sooty terns normally nest in their hundreds on the low-lying sandy beaches, but there were times when they would suddenly abandon their colony and fly inland. When they did, a severe tropical storm or hurricane was on its way. This earned them their name 'hurricane birds'.

Probably the most dramatic and memorable hurricane in recent years was Hurricane Andrew; in economic terms it was the most destructive hurricane ever to hit the USA. Andrew was born on 13 August 1992, a minor thunderstorm over west Africa. It did not have the honour of a name then, it was just one of hundreds of thunderstorms that form every year, most of them dissipating without further harm. This storm moved out into the Atlantic Ocean as an area of low pressure with rain and wind, but by 17 August it had grown enough to be recognized as a tropical storm and given a name.

Each tropical storm that forms in the Atlantic is given a name from the first half of the alphabet, starting with A at the beginning of each season. The names alternate between male and female. The storms in the Atlantic are monitored by the National Hurricane Centre at Coral Gables in Miami; it is here that they are named, their progress followed and decisions made about issuing warnings to the public.

Tropical Storm Andrew made its way across the Atlantic. By Friday 21 August, it was 1,600 km (1,000 miles) off the Florida coast and gathering strength. On Saturday 22 August, its sustained winds reached 120 kph (74 miles) per hour – Andrew had grown into a hurricane. It made its relentless progress towards the Florida coast, moving over warm water that was feeding the storm with the energy it needed to grow. A Hurricane Watch had been posted for the Florida coast from Vero Beach south to the Keys; by the evening of the Saturday this was scaled up to a full Hurricane Warning, breaking into the normal scheduled television programmes for the area.

On the morning of Sunday 23 August, it seemed there was no option but to evacuate. Beachfront properties were

slow descending air creates clear 'eye'

high level winds spiral outwards

spiral bands of thunderclouds

solid wall of cloud around 'eye'

warm tropical water

warm wet air drawn inwards

fast rising updrafts create thunderclouds

low pressure creates mound of water

rotation of storm

The anatomy of a hurricane

Hurricane Andrew crosses the Florida peninsula, August 1992

Predicting Hurricanes

The National Hurricane Centre, in Coral Gables, Miami, is the nerve centre that co-ordinates the monitoring and prediction of tropical storms and hurricanes. It is from here that the hurricane watches are organized and managed and warnings are issued, that the media are kept informed about approaching storms.

Jerry Jarrell is a meteorologist at the NHC who has worked with hurricanes most of his adult life. He lives in Miami, and his home was in the path of Hurricane Andrew in 1992. The forecasters at the NHC were continually monitoring the storm as it came closer. How do you prepare for an event like Andrew?

The media is a central part of the team. We don't try to exclude them, we try to bring them in if we can.'

The problem is in predicting the path of the storm accurately. If a warning to evacuate the area goes out, and it is a false alarm, the disruption and cost is enormous. But if the storm is approaching a built-up area they have to be sure that they evacuate the right people at the right time.

There are roughly two-thirds of a million people that should evacuate, that live close enough to the water that they really should evacuate. We think it would take about 24 hours to evacuate that number of people. There are another two or three million people in this area that probably should not evacuate. They live in homes that will keep them safe, and they will survive. They'll be terrified, but they'll survive. Now, if all those people tried to evacuate, then instead of 24 hours it may take three days or so.

Now the great fear is that you're going to have this huge traffic jam – gridlock – and then the hurricane comes and a car is much more dangerous to be in than a home. And now you're going to have people blown off

The National Hurricane Centre, Miami, Florida

the highway, because most of the roads they'll be on are elevated, and beside the highway is low-lying land, that's where the fill came from for the elevated road. That's going to be flooded and so we're afraid that in that kind of scenario you could lose hundreds – the only reason we don't say thousands is that we just can't bring ourselves to even imagine a thousand people, but it's certainly possible.

The ones that should evacuate are the ones that are along the coast. The storm surge can literally come up as much as 15 or 20 feet. So that means anything that's along the coast is subject to flooding, and that could be to the top of the first floor in most structures. And if they're within that first block they'll be subject to ocean waves and the battering action will destroy any building. So 90 per cent of the fatalities come from storm flooding.

boarded up, hotels emptied and closed. The only way out was north; on a Sunday afternoon, a quarter of a million people drove up the Florida turnpike, where the tolls were waived, and many of them headed to Orlando. The complex of hotels around Disneyworld were safely inland, and could absorb the wave of evacuees.

At the same time that south Florida was being evacuated, Andrew hit the Bahamas with wind speeds of 240 kph (150 mph), and killed four people. Moving on, still gathering strength over the warm water, Andrew slammed into the coast just south of Miami at 3 am on Monday 24 August. Those that had stayed experienced a night of rain and sus-

tained winds of 235 kph (145 mph); gusts were measured at 280 kph (175 mph). The noise was unimaginable – the roaring of the wind, the crashing and splintering as roofs were ripped off houses and structures torn apart. Andrew cut a swathe 40 km (25 miles) wide across southern Florida, with 300,000 homes in its path, and 80,000 of them were destroyed. Although there was a storm surge of 5 m (17 ft) that hit the coast, it swamped an area that was not highly developed. Most of Andrew's damage was done by the winds.

In Miami, the animals escaped from Dade County Metro Zoo. The small town of Homestead, south of Miami, was

Hurricanes Around the World

Although the word 'hurricane' is often applied to storms with exceptionally strong winds, hurricane is usually a severe tropical storm that forms under certain conditions.

Hurricanes are born on the edges of the Doldrums, the intertropical convergence zone, and in the Atlantic Ocean this area is usually to the north of the equator. They travel towards the west, blown by the Trade Winds, so the area most at risk is the Caribbean and the southeast coast of the USA. In the summer, the warm, relatively shallow waters of the Caribbean and the Gulf of Mexico provide the energy for tropical storms to turn into hurricanes, whereas later in the summer the water further out in the Atlantic has warmed enough for hurricanes to form further east.

Because the Doldrums are to the north of the equator, hurricanes rarely form in the south Atlantic. But in the Pacific Ocean, the Doldrums extend to the north and south of the equator; here, hurricanes are referred to by their other name, *typhoons*. The name comes from the Chinese *tai-fung*, meaning 'great wind'. Again, they tend to move towards the west because of the direction of the Trade Winds, so the areas at risk are Southeast Asia and the southwest Pacific, including Australia. The severe storms round the area of the Indian Ocean and Australia are referred to as *tropical cyclones*.

For a tropical storm to turn into a fully developed hurricane or typhoon is relatively rare; fewer than a hundred will form in a

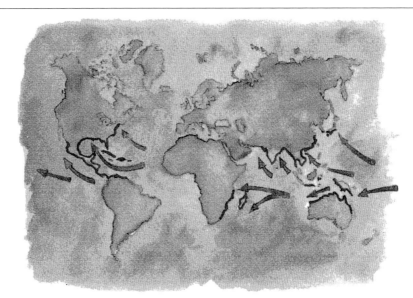

Regions vulnerable to hurricanes

typical year. Once the hurricane is born, it tends to move away from the equator; but hurricanes rarely reach latitudes more than 30° north or south of the tropics, as the water is not warm enough to sustain the huge energy demands of the storm.

A hurricane cannot cross the equator because the Coriolis effect does not apply here. The hurricane loses the energy it would otherwise gain from its rotation. If the hurricane does approach the equator, it eventually dissipates into bands of thunderstorms, then dies.

Hurricanes are renowned for their destructive power, but there have been times in history when they have seemed like a blessing. In the late thirteenth century, the Mongol emperor Kublai Khan was twice

stopped from attacking Japan with his imposing naval fleets by typhoons scattering and destroying his ships. To Japan, this was a sign that their country would be protected from invasion; they gave the name *kami-kaze* to the typhoon, meaning 'divine wind'.

Satellite images now allow weather forecasters to follow storms as they develop; the first signs will be a large cluster of thunderstorms, and if the images show that the system is beginning to rotate it will be watched carefully by meteorologists. Whereas in previous centuries a hurricane arrived without warning and could kill thousands of people, today the international system of weather-forecasting and communications can give enough warning to save lives, if not property.

annihilated. It was a residential community, with many immigrant workers, and their housing was substandard and, too often, building regulations had been ignored. All that was left was splintered wood; the power lines had been destroyed and the water supply disrupted. One woman stood among the wreckage, saying 'They're telling me to boil my drinking water – but I haven't anything to boil my water *on.*'

South Florida was declared a disaster area and the army was sent in to distribute blankets, food and basic provisions, organize the distribution of fresh water and stop looting. It would take Florida years to recover from Andrew. Meanwhile, as Andrew swept across the south of the peninsula, like all hurricanes over land it was cut off from its energy supply – the warm sea – and began to weaken. But the peninsula is only 160 km (100 miles) wide, and Andrew passed out into the Gulf of Mexico where it could once more feed off the sea's energy and recover its strength. Now it was heading for the coast of Louisiana, and the residents began to evacuate; it had built up to 200 kph (120 mph) winds. But when it hit the coast it did so where there was little settlement. Mangrove trees were battered and the water stirred up so much that millions of fish were suffocated. Fifteen people were killed, but, considering the violence of the storm, it was nothing short of a miracle that there were not many more casualties.

Andrew finally died over Louisiana with its last heavy rain over the Mississippi. But for the first time scientists were able to identify a new phenomenon, which explained the terrible destruction wreaked by the storm. The sustained winds that were rotating around the eye of the storm were spawning small, lethal vortices, only 150 m (500 ft) across, like eddies in a stream. As these vortices moved in towards the eye wall, they are stretched upwards, making them narrower and the winds faster. At the extreme, these vortices were only 24 m (80 ft) across, but with winds of 130 kph (80 mph). Add this wind speed to the wind of the hurricane itself, and an eddy can move along a very narrow track, blowing at over 320 kph (200 mph). When Andrew passed through, one eddy could demolish one side of a street and leave the other side intact.

A fast, twisting column of air does not only occur inside a hurricane. It can be created on the outside edge of a dying hurricane and take on a life of its own, or it can form when a downdraught of air from a thunderstorm starts to spin. A hurricane may be the most powerful storm on the planet, but the most deadly, the most chaotic, the most capricious is the tornado.

Tornadoes usually form from the vertical movement of air in a deep layer of cloud, as in a thunderstorm. A rotating column of air forms within the cloud, and as the rate of spin increases the tornado reaches downwards from the base of the cloud. Even today, radar information can only give a few minutes' warning, just long enough to dive for cover in a tornado shelter – if there is one. Only a few hundred metres across, the twister moves on a meandering path at up to 100 kph (65 mph), but it packs winds of over 400 kph (250 mph). Not only that, but the lifting effect of the low pressure can pick up cars and trucks, and the difference in pressure as it passes through can cause a building to explode. And all this can be over in a matter of minutes, the twister dissipating as fast as it formed, leaving behind a trail of death and destruction. Hundreds of people are killed each year by tornadoes; the vicious winds can turn gravel into gunshot, a pebble into a bullet, broken glass into unthinkable weapons of destruction.

We can now watch a hurricane form on satellite monitors before our very eyes, and, with advances in technology, we can predict its path with greater accuracy and reliability. But a twister seems to come from nowhere, and defeats all our attempts to resist it. With luck we may be able to outrun it, or we can hide underground and wait for it to pass. Yet, much as we are threatened by the destructive power of these storms, they are crucial to the smooth running of the planet. They release energy as it builds up, transferring heat from the ocean to the atmosphere, the safety valves in the system that is the Earth's atmosphere.

The aftermath of Hurricane Andrew, 1992

Right: **A 'twister' – the tornado reaches down to touch the Earth**

THE BIG WINDS

PART THREE
SUN AND MOON

Following the Sun

chapter 11

But I am constant as the northern star,

Of whose true-fixed and resting quality

There is no fellow in the firmament.

The skies are painted with unnumbered sparks,

They are all fire and every one does shine

But there's one in all doth hold his place.

Julius Caesar – *William Shakespeare*

The passage of time seems inevitable; we are always aware of that passage of time because we can see changes around us. Probably the first changes that our ancestors noticed were the changes in light and dark, night and day, warm and cold – the seasons. They did not know that the Earth was a sphere, spinning on its axis and orbiting the sun. They only knew that day followed night, that the sun appeared and disappeared, that the moon changed shape with a pattern of its own, that the weather changed and that the length of day varied over a period of a year.

The Earth *is* shaped like a ball, slightly flattened at the poles, spinning about an axis through the north and south poles. As it spins, there is always somewhere on the planet experiencing day and somewhere experiencing night. Dawn sweeps across the face of the Earth at 1,600 kph

(1,000 mph), appearing to move westwards as the planet turns from west to east.

But the length of day and night is not the same all over the planet, and it also varies throughout the year as the seasons change. Sometimes the day is longer than the night and we experience the warmth of summer, sometimes the night is longer than the day and we experience the cold of winter. And *all* these effects are explained by one simple fact about the Earth. *The Earth is tilted on its axis.*

There is often confusion about this. Various misunderstandings arise; for example, the fact that the Earth's orbit round the sun is not an exact circle means that for part of the year the Earth is slightly closer to the sun than the rest of the time. But this effect is negligible when it comes to explaining the seasons; the *only* reason we have such extreme seasons is because of the Earth's tilt.

To explain further. The Earth and all the planets orbit the sun in one plane, as if they are on a flat disc; if we

Changing colours mark the turning of the seasons

watch the night sky, the planets all appear to move along a band, parallel to the path of the sun across the sky. This path is called the *ecliptic*. It is as if we see the 'disc' edge-on; the sun and the planets seem to move along a band of stars recognized by the pattern of their constellations; this is the *zodiac*. The constellations are named after animals, hence 'zoo'. These 12 constellations give their names to the signs of the zodiac, and the sun passes through each of the 12 signs once a year, entering a new sign roughly on the 21st of the month. For readers of popular horoscopes, this gives us our 'sun sign', so that if we are born on, say, 10 August, then the sun will be in the sign of Leo; on 19 October it will be in Libra, and so on.

The Earth is spinning at the same time as it orbits the sun. If the Earth's axis was at a right angle to the line between the Earth and the sun, we would have no seasons. But the Earth's axis is tilted over at an angle of about 23 degrees, so sometimes the north pole is tipped towards the sun, sometimes away from it.

The Earth's axis always points in the same direction as it travels round the sun; its orientation in space does not seem to change. For our purposes, the north pole always points to the same position in space, and, looking at the night sky, we can identify that point as the star Polaris or the 'pole star'.

To understand the changing year, it will help to look at what happens during the day. The sun rises in the morning and climbs higher in the sky, until, at midday, it is as high as it will go. If it is not cloudy, and we can see our shadow, it will be at its shortest at noon. Then the sun sinks, getting lower in the sky, until it sets in the evening. But we also know that, as the year passes, the days get longer and then shorter again, and the midday sun is much higher in summer than it is at noon on a winter's day.

This change in the sun's passage across the sky is tied to the changing length of daylight – and the different seasons. The cycle of the year is continuous, but, to explain why it changes, we need to join in with it somewhere – it does not matter much where.

So, if we look at the time when the Earth is at its position when the North Pole is tipped towards the sun, the northern hemisphere is experiencing summer. At this exact moment, everywhere north of the equator experiences the longest day and shortest night; this is Midsummer Day, otherwise known as the *summer solstice*. It occurs on or around 21 June every year.

As we approach the summer solstice, every day the position of the midday sun gets higher and higher in the sky, until at the solstice it seems to stop changing for a few days. The sun will rise to the north of east and set to the north of west; it is in the sky for the longest time, giving us our longest day. After the solstice, as the days pass, the midday sun is not so high, and the days are not so long. The word 'solstice' comes from 'sol' and 'stasis'; in other words, the 'sun stands still'. It refers to the fact that over the few days around the solstice the length of day and position of the midday sun do not change.

Meanwhile, the southern hemisphere is experiencing winter, as the south pole is pointing away from the sun, so the nights are longer than the days, and with less sun the climate is cold. The southern hemisphere experiences winter during the months of May, June, July and August.

But the Earth continues its journey round the sun, and as it does the days start to get shorter; the sun rises later and sets earlier. Eventually, three months after the summer solstice, around 21 September, we reach a time when the night and day are of equal length, with 12 hours of daylight and 12 hours of darkness. We have now reached the *autumn equinox*, and everywhere on the globe receives the same amount of light and dark. It is *only* on the equinox that the sun rises exactly due east and sets exactly due west. Now the Earth's axis is 'side-on' to the sun and neither north nor south pole points towards the sun. This is a major turning point of the year, because as the Earth sweeps past this crucial point the North Pole starts to point away from the sun, and the days in the northern hemisphere are getting shorter than the nights. In other words, the 'nights are drawing in'.

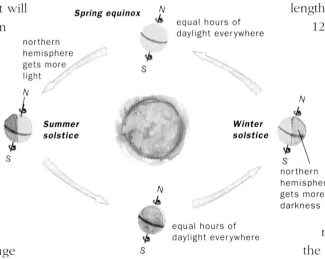

Spring equinox

equal hours of daylight everywhere

northern hemisphere gets more light

Summer solstice

Winter solstice

northern hemisphere gets more darkness

equal hours of daylight everywhere

Autumn equinox

Generating the seasons

The sun now rises to the south of east and sets to the south of west, and the length of daylight gets shorter and shorter. Receiving less sunlight each day, the temperature drops and the cold of winter grips the northern hemisphere. But now the South Pole is pointing towards the sun, so the southern hemisphere is basking in sunlight. In the months of October, November, December, and January, the southern hemisphere enjoys summer, and Australians may celebrate Christmas with a barbecue on the beach. Eventually, three months after the autumn equinox, the Earth reaches the position where the North Pole is pointing directly away from the sun and the South Pole towards it. This is the shortest day in the north, around 21 December, the winter solstice. In the days around the winter solstice, the midday sun is as low in the sky as it is going to get, and

Deciduous trees shed their leaves at the start of winter

the sun rises as far south east and sets as far south west as it can. Again, the sun's position each day at noon stays the same for a few days, and we have reached another turning point in the seasons. Once the winter solstice has passed, the days in the north start to get longer, the sun rises earlier and sets later, and spring is on its way.

Moving on another three months after the winter solstice, the Earth reaches a second point in its journey where everywhere on the globe again receives equal hours of light and darkness. We have reached the *spring equinox*, or as it sometimes called, the *vernal equinox*. The sun rises exactly due east and sets in the west, and, once the spring equinox has passed, the northern hemisphere gets warmer, the days get longer, and three months later we are back where we started, at the summer solstice.

The naming of the seasons and the points of the year were first made in Europe and the East, in the northern hemisphere, so that the descriptions for the whole globe are somewhat biased. We still tend to refer to the 'spring equinox' and 'autumn equinox' from the northern perspective.

Although the Earth's journey round the sun explains the seasons and the changing day length, the actual variation in light and temperature also depends on exactly *where* we are on the Earth. It not only changes with the time of year, it changes with how far north or south of the equator we are, in other words with *latitude*. For everyone who has not picked up an atlas since geography lessons at school, latitude is a handy way of measuring the position north or south of the equator. Taking the equator as 0°, latitude is measured in degrees north or south, as if someone was standing at the centre of the Earth and measuring the angle between you and the equator. The North Pole will then be 90° north, and the South Pole will be 90° south, with everywhere else somewhere in between.

We know that around the equator, in the band we refer to as the 'tropics', it is usually hot, and at the poles it is usually cold. But what exactly are the 'tropics'? We come back to the tilt of the Earth and the changing seasons again. For anyone living on the equator, as anywhere else, at the spring and autumn equinoxes there is equal light and darkness, but at the equator the noon sun would be directly overhead. If we stood out in the sunshine at midday, we would have no shadow. But, as we have seen, after the spring equinox the Earth moves so that the North Pole is pointing towards the sun, so the northern hemisphere gets more sunlight than the south. Now, the midday sun appears to be directly overhead further and further north, until at the summer solstice it is as far north as it seems to get.

Once the summer solstice has passed, the noon sun will only appear directly overhead further south, until at the equinox it is directly over the equator. So there is a limit to how far north we can see the noon sun directly overhead; any further north, it can never be directly overhead. This limit is given a name, it is the *Tropic of Cancer*, and, in the same way as the equator is a circle round the Earth that has a latitude of 0°, the Tropic of Cancer is a circle round the Earth with a latitude of roughly 23°. Its name comes from the position of the sun at the summer solstice; on 21 June the sun enters the zodiac sign of Cancer.

Similarly, the place the furthest south that has the sun directly overhead at noon is a circle with a latitude of 23° south, which is called the *Tropic of Capricorn*; the sun enters the sign of Capricorn on the winter solstice, on 21 December. So everywhere between the Tropic of Cancer and the Tropic of Capricorn is referred to as 'the tropics'; sometime during the year the sun will be directly overhead at all the places in the tropics.

Although the temperature does not alter much in this band, there *are* seasons, but, rather than warm and cold, the seasons are wet and dry. The periods of rain depend on the movement of the intertropical convergence zone – the Doldrums – the band of warm, wet air round the equator. This band moves north and south as the Earth's tilt creates the seasons, moving north in the northern summer and south in the winter. This band brings the rain, so places in the tropics near the equator have two wet and two dry seasons as it passes over and back again. This seasonal change in rain and drought drives one of the great spectacles of the natural world. In Africa, huge herds of game animals follow the rains, where the fresh, new grass will grow. Millions of wildebeest, zebra and antelopes all respond to the tropical seasons, spending most of their lives on great journeys covering hundreds, if not thousands of kilometres. They are searching for food, but, in doing so, they are responding to the great rhythms created by the Earth's own journey round the sun.

That the Earth is tilted on its axis has a crucial effect on our daily lives, but this still leaves the question as to *why* it is tilted. The answer lies in the Earth's turning about its axis; it behaves like a child's spinning top. When a top is wound up far enough, and spins fast enough, it does so with its axis upright on the floor. But eventually it starts to slow down, and as it does it begins to wobble, in slow circles, getting lower and lower until it finally tumbles to the ground. The Earth is exactly like a top; initially it was spinning with its axis upright on the 'floor', the plane of the solar system. But the spinning is slowing down – much too slowly for us to notice – and like a top, the Earth is wobbling.

So the Earth tilts because, like the child's spinning top, it is slowley winding down and tipping over. And each wobble takes 26,000 years. Although the North Pole points to the star Polaris now, it has not always done so, and, in time, will point somewhere else.

The first young spring flowers emerge before the new leaves cast a shadow on the forest floor

The Zodiac

The zodiac is a particular band of constellations that stretches across the night sky, and that lies on the path of the planets – the 'wanderers', as the ancients called them. They were named after the animals that the patterns of stars seemed to represent; these 12 constellations give their names to the 'signs of the zodiac' so beloved of newspapers and magazines.

But the spinning Earth behaves like a child's top that wobbles as it begins to slow down. In the same way, the Earth's axis wobbles, so that its axis points in a different direction over a 26,000-year cycle. This effect is called the *precession of the equinoxes* and seems to play havoc with the idea of the zodiac. The signs of the zodiac were created when the patterns were identified and named well over 2,000 years ago. At that point, the sun would enter each of the constellations on the dates that we now use when we find our 'sun sign'; on 21 March, on the spring equinox, the sun enters the sign of Aries, on 21 April it enters the sign of Taurus, and so on.

Yet in the 2,000 years since these constellations were identified, the precession of the equinoxes means that the star patterns that defined these signs has slipped backwards. The constellations no longer match up with the dates that are given for the sun signs. When the sun is said to be in the sign of Leo, between 21 July and 21 August, it is actually against the star pattern of the constellation of Cancer. So how do astrologers deal with this discrepancy? Although the sun signs in the magazines and newspapers carry little weight, the number of serious, professional astrologers is growing, and people are turning to them more and more. Yet the precession of the equinoxes cannot be ignored.

The answer is that there are two zodiacs, the *tropical zodiac* and the *sidereal zodiac*. The tropical zodiac is the system that is used to allocate the signs starting with Aries at 21 March. It is not as arbitrary as it seems, as this system is based on the seasons, with the main four points of the year being the equinoxes and the solstices. The sidereal zodiac or 'star zodiac' is a system of working with the positions of the sun and planets against the constellations as they are now.

Most professional astrologers use the tropical zodiac. The reason for this is that the changes in the seasons here on Earth are more immediate in our lives than the distant stars. The nature of the different signs is determined by where in the year the sign occurs, whether at the beginning of spring, the height of summer, or the depths of winter. The precession of the equinoxes was observed by Hipparchus – born in 190 BC – who defined the tropical and sidereal zodiacs. It was known even then, during the times when it was thought that the flat Earth was the centre of the universe.

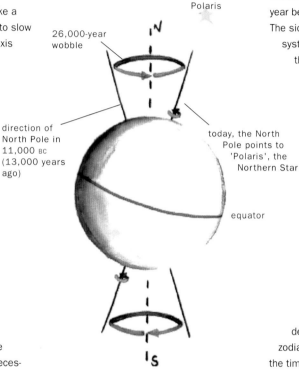

Polaris

26,000-year wobble

N

direction of North Pole in 11,000 BC (13,000 years ago)

today, the North Pole points to 'Polaris', the Northern Star

equator

S

The precession of the equinoxes

This effect is called the precession of the equinoxes. Over thousands of years, as the Earth wobbles, the position of the sun against the stars on the spring equinox, 21 March, gradually slips backwards. The sun's light is so bright that we cannot see the background of stars during the day, but, if we could, we would see the sun's position against the constellations. The position of the sun against these stars on 21 March is also called the 'First Point of Aries', because when the stars were first observed, 4,000 years ago, the sun was entering the constellation of Aries

Seasonal changes of rain and drought in the tropics drive migrations of millions of wildebeest

the Ram on this day, the spring equinox. But as the Earth wobbles, the direction to which it points changes, so now the sun is actually between the constellations of Aquarius and Pisces on this date. This point is gradually moving from Pisces to Aquarius, and this is the origin of the 'Age of Aquarius' that is the hallmark of the New Age. The sun stays in each constellation for just over 2,000 years. So the night sky that our ancestors watched would be unrecognizable to us now; the familiar stars and patterns would have either disappeared or be in a different position. Shakespeare's northern star would not be where he expected it to be; it will only take another 26,000 years before the sky once more looks the same.

chapter 12

The Moon

Slowly, silently, now the moon

Walks the night in her silver shoon.

'Silver' – *Walter de la Mare*

For a dead lump of rock orbiting the Earth, the moon has inspired more stories, myths, prayers and rituals than anything else in human history. She is a mighty huntress who rules the night sky, Diana. She is the changing face of the Celtic threefold goddess, the Morrigan, her phases of virgin, mother and crone reflected in the crescent, full and waning moon. She was a great mother, the monthly phases showing her changes in fertility, swelling in her pregnancy, and giving birth; she was also the destroyer, disappearing into darkness for three days each month.

To the Egyptians, the moon was male, who could become an old man or a child as he pleased. He was worshipped as the god Thoth, and he was also the god Osiris, who died and was reborn when his wife Isis brought the remains of his body together.

The connection between the 28 days of the moon's cycle and the menstrual cycle of women has always linked the moon to fertility, whether the deity was male or female. Even when the moon seems to disappear completely at the

The ballet of the Earth, moon and sun creates the rhythms of the days, months and years

end of the cycle, it always appears again, the cycle seeming to be unbreakable. It is this eternally changing face of the moon that has commanded such fascination for thousands of years of human history.

The Earth is the only one of the 'terrestrial', inner planets to have a moon; only the huge gas giants – Jupiter, Saturn, Uranus, and Neptune – share this privilege. There is much and varied discussion as to where our moon came from; we do know that it is the same age as the Earth. One of the possible explanations is that a huge impact with the Earth – from maybe a large meteor – caused debris and material to explode into space. This material was left orbiting the Earth and, in the same way the planets formed around the sun, the fragments came together by the process of accretion, forming our satellite.

The moon is much smaller than the Earth; its diameter would just about fit on the North American continent. Its gravitational effect is much less, so whatever we may weigh on Earth we would seem to weigh only a fifth of that if we were on the moon's surface. If the moon ever did have an atmosphere, its gravity was not strong enough to hold onto

Buzz Aldrin – the second man on the moon

it, so it would have escaped into space. With no atmosphere, there has been no weathering or erosion. The footprints that Neil Armstrong left in the dust are still the same today. In a similar way, the moon holds a record of every impact with every meteor that hit it; some were enormous, some were microscopic, but they all left their mark on the surface.

Apart from the sun, the moon is the most obvious light in the sky. Astrologers called these stars 'Lights' or 'Luminaries' but whereas sunlight floods the sky, creating the day, even the full moon only just casts enough light to throw a shadow. We see it shine at night because it reflects the light of the sun, but its dead, rocky surface only reflects a fraction – 7 per cent – of the light it receives. This is about the same reflectivity as coal dust.

The Earth, sun and moon perform a complex ballet that affects us every day. The moon orbits the Earth once every 27 days, 7 hours, 43 minutes and 11.5 seconds, and as it does the amount that is lit by the sun – that we can see on Earth – changes. When the moon is on the same side of the Earth as the sun, it is in the sky during the day and the

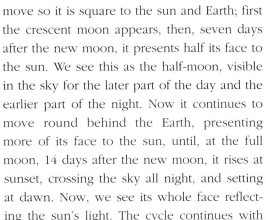

Neil Armstrong's footprint

sun's light is behind it, so we cannot see it. This is the dark time, the new moon, when the only light in the night sky comes from the stars.

As it passes on its journey round the Earth, it begins to move so it is square to the sun and Earth; first the crescent moon appears, then, seven days after the new moon, it presents half its face to the sun. We see this as the half-moon, visible in the sky for the later part of the day and the earlier part of the night. Now it continues to move round behind the Earth, presenting more of its face to the sun, until, at the full moon, 14 days after the new moon, it rises at sunset, crossing the sky all night, and setting at dawn. Now, we see its whole face reflecting the sun's light. The cycle continues with the moon moving round behind the Earth, until once more only half its face appears lit and, 29 days, 12 hours, 44 minutes and 2.8 seconds later, it is once more between the Earth and the sun, a new moon.

With no erosion, dust on the moon's surface has lain undisturbed for millions of years

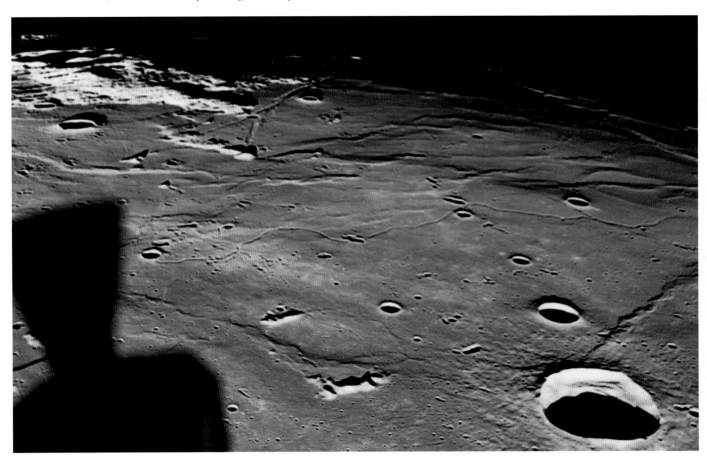

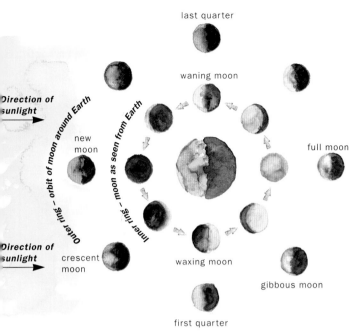

last quarter

waning moon

Direction of sunlight →

new moon

Outer ring – orbit of moon around Earth

Inner ring – moon as seen from Earth

full moon

Direction of sunlight →

crescent moon

waxing moon

gibbous moon

first quarter

The phases of the moon

The discrepancy between the time it takes to orbit the Earth and the time between two positions in its cycle, say between new moons, is due to the fact that the Earth has moved slightly on its path round the sun during the month it takes for the moon to make its orbit, so their relative positions will have changed slightly. But the moon also takes about 29 and a half days to rotate on its own axis, its own 'day-night' cycle, as it were. So it rotates at the same rate as it orbits the Earth, which means it always keeps the same face towards us. We could not even glimpse the other side of the moon until the space programme put satellites – and humans – in orbit round our own satellite.

When the Earth and moon line up in a straight line with the sun, as in the full moon and the new moon, the question arises as to why they do not get in each other's shadow. The answer is that sometimes they do, and when they do, they create an *eclipse*.

The moon's orbit is at a slight angle to the ecliptic, the path the sun and planets take across the sky. Most of the time, this slight tilt to the moon's orbit means that although it may line up with the sun and Earth, it is still clear of possible shadows. But if the moon crosses the ecliptic a new or full moon will produce an eclipse. This is where the word 'ecliptic' comes from; if the moon is also on the sun's path, an eclipse can occur.

When the moon comes between the sun and Earth, it

would normally produce a new moon. But when the moon is exactly on the ecliptic we experience a *solar eclipse*, where the sun's light is blocked. Although the sun is thousands of times bigger than the moon, the moon is so much closer to us that it appears that its disc is roughly the same size as that of the sun. So when the moon's disc completely covers the sun's disc, we have a *total eclipse*; if it only partly covers the sun's disc, we have a *partial eclipse*. When a total eclipse does occur, and the sky grows dark during the day, it is unsettling and seems as if the whole natural order of things has been disrupted, as if the constancy of the universe has fallen apart. The ancient astrologers and priests who could predict an eclipse were believed to wield a magical power.

When the moon is on the ecliptic on the *far* side of the Earth, the Earth blocks the sun's light, so instead of a full moon the shadow creates a lunar eclipse. Because the Earth is so much bigger than the moon, its shadow completely swallows the moon and a *lunar eclipse* can be seen everywhere on the Earth. The outline of the moon can still be made out, but it turns a dark, blood red.

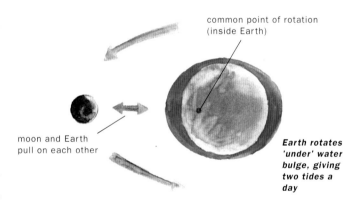

common point of rotation (inside Earth)

moon and Earth pull on each other

Earth rotates 'under' water bulge, giving two tides a day

The moon's phases are created by its movement around the Earth

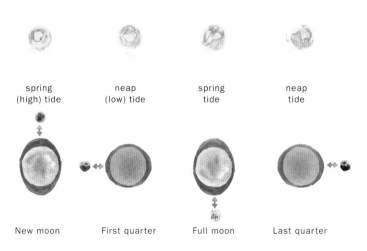

spring (high) tide	neap (low) tide	spring tide	neap tide
New moon	First quarter	Full moon	Last quarter

The Earth and moon pull on each other to create the tides

Eclipses and Shadows

A lunar eclipse occurs when the moon is on the far side of the Earth from the sun, so that the shadow of the Earth falls on the moon and it does not reflect the sun's light. But the Earth's shadow is made up of two parts, the *umbra* and the *penumbra*, and depending on which part of the shadow falls on the moon the effect is slightly different.

The *umbra* is the long, cone-shaped shadow of the Earth that extends into space, but around the umbra is the *penumbra*, an area of partial shadow, whereby only some of the sun's light is blocked. When the moon passes into the Earth's shadow, it first passes into the penumbra, when its surface becomes darker but is still visible. If then only a part of the moon passes into the umbra, only this part will be in total shadow, creating a *partial eclipse*. It can look very much as if something has taken a bite out of the moon.

For a total eclipse of the moon, the whole moon must pass into umbra. If it passes through the centre, the eclipse lasts roughly two hours, but the moon can just dip into and out of the umbra, giving a much shorter eclipse.

When a solar eclipse occurs, the moon creates the shadow which falls onto the Earth. In the same way as the Earth, the moon has the full shadow, the umbra, and the partial shadow, the penumbra. The moon

Lunar eclipse (visible during night)

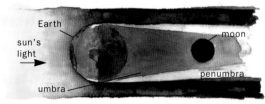

Solar eclipse (visible during day)

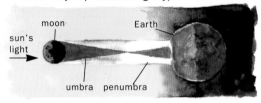

Solar (annular) eclipse

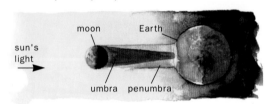

Solar and Lunar eclipses

is much smaller than the Earth, and therefore casts a smaller shadow; it is only when the Earth passes into the umbra part

of the shadow that a total eclipse occurs. Where the umbra touches the face of the Earth, it is actually only 269 km (167 miles) wide, or less, so that the total eclipse can only be seen in a very small area on the Earth's surface.

As the moon does not move round the Earth in an exact circle, sometimes the moon is slightly further away from the Earth when the eclipse occurs. In this case, the moon's disc does not completely cover that of the sun, so an *annular eclipse* is seen – a ring of bright sunlight around the dark moon. When this happens, the umbra has not reached as far as the Earth at all.

In a total eclipse, the shadow moves across the surface of the Earth as the planet is rotating, and the moon is also moving around the Earth. This means the eclipse can only be seen for a brief period, a matter of minutes; the maximum length of time it will be visible is only seven and a half minutes.

If the moon's orbit was in exactly the same plane as the Earth's orbit round the sun, instead of a new moon and full moon every month, there would be solar and lunar eclipse. It is because the moon's orbit is tilted at 5° to that of the Earth's that eclipses happen so infrequently.

Apart from bringing a light to the night sky, the moon also affects the oceans in ways that dominate the lives of those of us who live by the sea. It creates the tides.

Roughly twice a day the sea level rises and falls, a high tide and low tide, a constant rhythm that has no connection to day or night. In some places in the world, like the Mediterranean, the tide is almost negligible, only a metre or so; in other places, like the English Channel, it can be as much as 20 m (65 ft). Fishermen and people of the shore, whose lives were lived around the moods of the sea, knew about tides and understood their patterns. But it was not until Isaac Newton proposed his theory of gravity, in 1687, that it was understood that the tides were a result of the moon's gravitational pull on the Earth.

As we saw in the beginning, gravity is a force that acts on both bodies in question; the Earth pulled the apple towards it, but the apple also pulled on the Earth. And this same force, gravity, keeps the moon in its orbit round the Earth and the Earth in orbit round the sun. If we have an object on a piece of string we can swing it in a circle – the string keeps the object from flying off, but if it moves fast enough, it traces a circle. On a different scale, in space, it is gravity that keeps the moon from 'flying off', but the moon's motion round the Earth is fast enough to stop it just falling towards Earth like the apple.

As we swing our object on the string, we can feel the pull of the string on our fingers; in the same way, the moon swinging round the Earth pulls on the Earth. This pull does not have an obvious effect on the land, but it does affect all the water; the oceans are free to slosh around, and so are pulled towards the moon, making a bulge on that side of the Earth. The Earth spins on its axis 'under' this bulge, so the sea level rises and falls as the Earth turns. But if it were this simple there would be one high tide and one low tide a day, not two.

However, the Earth is also attracted to the moon, and although we think of the moon going round the Earth they are actually going round each other, orbiting a common point like a dumbbell. It is just that the Earth is so much bigger than the moon that the common point is inside the Earth, so the moon traces a larger circle. If we replace our object on a string with a bucket on a rope, and put water in the bucket, we can still swing it round, even swing it overhead, and if the motion is fast enough the water stays in the bucket. In the same way, some of the sea is forced away from the Earth on the opposite side to the moon, so, in all, this movement creates two bulges, one each side of the Earth, and hence giving two tides a day.

Many creatures live their lives governed by the rise and fall of the tides rather than the pattern of night and day. Shore birds feed on exposed mudflats at low tide, and when the tide comes in they move to higher ground to roost, waiting for the tide to go out again. On the island of Herm, in the English Channel Islands, when the tide goes

Walking on the Moon

It was a moment when everyone on the Earth held their breath and watched. The moment when a human first stood on another world. At 10.56 pm Eastern Daylight Time, on 20 July 1969, Neil Armstrong stepped out of the lunar module, at the edge of the Sea of Tranquillity, and his words would become immortal: 'That's one small step for a man, one giant leap for mankind.'

He was joined on the moon's surface by Buzz Aldrin, and the two of them spent more than two hours walking, setting up experiments, collecting samples of dust and rocks, and setting up the American 'Stars and Stripes', braced to hang as if flying even though there was no atmosphere. Their every move was monitored back on Earth, and they chatted to the president, Richard Nixon, in the White House. When they had finished they returned to the lunar module, and took off their heavy, bulky spacesuits to rest for a few hours before taking off. They rejoined the command and service module that had stayed in orbit round the moon, piloted by Michael Collins, and the three men returned safely to Earth. The whole expedition had taken them seven days.

The first moon landing was the culmination of the space race, that had been set in action by John F. Kennedy, when he promised in 1961 that 'by the end of the decade, we will have put a man on the moon and brought him safely back to Earth.'

The programme of unmanned space flight and manned expeditions had not been without its disasters. In 1967, on 27 January, three men died on the launch pad as a flash fire engulfed the cockpit; the deaths of Grissom, White and Chaffee set back the *Apollo* programme by a year as the cause of the accident was investigated. But in 1968 *Apollo 10* took three men to orbit the moon, and Stafford and Cernan transferred to a lunar module and took it to within 16 km (10 miles) of the moon's surface, before reuniting with the command module, piloted by Young, and returning to Earth, having completed the rehearsal for the moon landing itself.

The series of moon landings that began with *Apollo 11* would continue until 1972. In 1970, the crew of the unlucky *Apollo 13* had to be brought back to Earth having not made the landing, as an oxygen tank had exploded. Between them, the astronauts and the team at mission control used every ingenious trick they could to bring the men back in one piece, as much of a triumph as the moon landing itself.

Apollo 17 was the last expedition to the moon, in December 1972. After that, most of the USA space effort went into the Space Shuttle. But in January 1998 an unmanned probe was sent to the moon; its mission was to search for ice that might be lurking in the depths of craters on the dark side. If ice was there, it could provide a water supply for our future visits to our moon.

The Lunar Excursion Module approaching the surface of the moon, July 1996

out the sands turn a brilliant emerald green. Tiny flatworms live in the sand and come out at low tide to sunbathe. They are green – and need the sunlight – because of what lives inside them. Algae provide energy by photosynthesis, making food from carbon dioxide, water and sunlight; the flatworms live on the energy provided by the algae. They retreat into the sands as the high tide comes in so they are not exposed to hungry fish.

Although the moon is the main force in creating the tides, the sun's gravity does have some effect. When there is a new moon or a full moon, the sun and moon are lined up and the sun's gravity reinforces that of the moon. This creates higher tides than usual, *spring tides*, that happen twice a month. The tide is more extreme; the high water is higher than normal and low tide is lower than normal. But when the sun and moon are square to each other relative to the Earth, at the first or third quarter, they have the effect of partly cancelling out each other's gravity. The tides are not as high as normal; the high tide is not so high and the low tide not so low. These weaker tides are the *neap tides* and also occur twice a month.

The power of the moon to move vast amounts of water can be seen when a spring tide creates a *bore*. Some river estuaries are shaped like funnels, so when the tide comes in the water is forced into an even narrower channel. This effect is even more pronounced on the spring tide, when so much water is forced inland that a wall of water sweeps upstream, overriding the normal flow of the river. The height of this wave of water will depend on several factors, including the amount of water flowing downstream in the river, so will not be identical on every spring tide. There are several river estuaries in the world where this happens. The river Seine in France has a tidal bore which is called the 'mascaret', and another forms on the Petitcodiac River which flows into the Bay of Fundy in New Brunswick.

A famous bore sweeps up the river Severn in England. It is funnelled up the Bristol Channel and into the narrower part of the river, where a wave over 1 m (3 ft) high passes up the river, as far as the city of Gloucester, 50 km (30 miles) or so upstream; the bore is only stopped by lock gates on the river. It is an event watched by people who wait on the bank for the bore to pass, and a few hardy souls even surf the wave.

On the other side of the Atlantic Ocean, on the eastern coast of the USA, an ancient creature leaves the safety of the ocean on the spring tides. Horseshoe crabs emerge onto

the sandy beaches in spring and summer to lay their eggs, just below the high tide mark. These large crabs, up to 60 cm (2 ft) in length, are more closely related to spiders than crabs, and they have been around for a very long time – over 500 million years. When they first laid their eggs on the beach, it was a safe place to leave them as there was no life to speak of on land.

But life has moved on since then. Now, thousands of shore birds – gulls, grackles, and even local pigeons, sparrows and starlings – come to gorge themselves on the millions of eggs left by the horseshoe crabs; one female can lay up to 80,000 eggs. So many eggs are laid by the thousands of crabs that invade the beach that enough will survive to produce the next generation. But the birds know when to come; often they arrive on the spring tide *before* the crabs have left the water. Like the ancient creatures of the sea, the birds are responding to the ancient rhythms that drive life on the planet.

Horseshoe crabs come ashore on the spring tide to spawn in Delaware Bay, on North America's Atlantic coast

Ice and Snow

chapter 13

There is only one great thing to live, to see...the great

day that dawns and the light that fills the world.

old Inuit song

The most isolated, cold, remote, windswept regions of the world are at the two poles. At the North Pole, the Arctic region has a sea at its centre covered by a permanent icesheet. At the South Pole, the huge continent of Antarctica is also covered by ice; it is the only continent that has never been colonized by humans.

Both polar regions are dominated by ice and snow, and there are but two seasons; light and dark. Summers are short, and the winters are long, and for life to survive at either pole is an ordeal. So why are these regions so extreme? There are several reasons, mostly to do with the tilt of the Earth on its axis that we met when looking at the seasons. Although half of the Earth always faces the sun and is bathed in sunlight, at the tropics all the sunlight reaches the surface from directly overhead. The nearer we are to the polar areas, the further away from the equator, the more the sun's light is slanted, reaching the surface at an angle. The same amount of sunlight is spread over a larger area than at the tropics, so it has less effect. At the poles themselves, the sunlight almost skims the surface, warming the ground less than the sun at the equator.

The polar regions get less of the sun's warmth than the tropics, but they are also affected more dramatically by the

Cold and remote – the windswept Arctic

seasons. In the northern hemisphere, in the summer, the further north we travel the longer the days and the shorter the nights. When we reach the Arctic regions – the northern extremes of Canada, Alaska, Greenland, Scandinavia and Siberia – the daylight gets longer and longer, and beyond a certain latitude, near Midsummer Day, the sun will not set at all. The 'certain latitude' is the Arctic Circle, a circle that has its equivalent in the far south as the Antarctic Circle. Everywhere *on* the Arctic Circle, on midsummer night, the sun does not set, it just skims the horizon. As we go further and further north of the Arctic Circle, the sun stays in the sky for longer and longer. There are more and more of these 'white nights', with their endless hours of daylight, before and after Midsummer Day. We have entered the 'Land of the Midnight Sun'.

The Arctic region is usually considered to be everywhere north of the Arctic Circle, and includes the Arctic Ocean, an ocean surrounded by Canada, Greenland, Siberia, Alaska and islands such as Svalbaard and Iceland. The ocean is open to the Atlantic at a gap between Greenland and Scandinavia, but otherwise the gaps between the landmasses are narrow, so the ocean is almost entirely enclosed. It is covered by a permanently frozen sheet of ice floating on the water.

The Arctic region qualifies as a desert because so little precipitation falls here as either rain or snow – less than

250 mm (10 in) a year. But, although the land is not always covered in snow and ice, there is always a layer of *permafrost*, a permanently frozen layer of ground up to 600 m (2,000 ft) deep. Building on permafrost is hazardous; if the structure is not insulated properly, it can melt the permafrost underneath, creating subsidence and even collapse.

Huge, treeless plains, *tundra*, stretch across northern Canada and Siberia. They are covered in low plants that can survive the low temperatures and dry conditions, such as lichens and mosses. Animals that live in the Arctic have also adapted to the cold. Polar bears, Arctic foxes and the Arctic wolf all have white fur as camouflage against the snow, and very thick coats insulate them against the freezing wind.

Polar bears are as much at home in the water as on land, and they are strong swimmers, often found great distances from land. They live mainly by hunting seals, but will also eat seaweed, fish, birds and caribou. The polar bear is hunted by the Inuit people of the Arctic for its flesh, fat and hide, but its liver, often a rich source of nutrition in many hunted animals, is inedible; it is poisonous to us because it contains a high level of vitamin A. Some polar bears hibernate, digging or finding a hole in the snow, but others are active throughout the long winter.

The people of the Arctic region live mainly by hunting and fishing. The Saami people of Scandinavia and the Nenets of Siberia follow the wild reindeer herds, herding them and using their carcasses and hides to provide food, clothing, tents and tools. The Eskimo, or Inuit people live in Canada, Greenland and the northeast of Siberia. There is much confusion over the name. 'Inuit' is the name meaning 'the real people', whereas 'Eskimo' was thought to be applied to them in the sixteenth century, by others, often said to mean 'eaters of raw fish'. Nowadays, the Arctic people of Alaska tend to call themselves Eskimo, while the others use 'Inuit', although there is no firm rule.

As everywhere on the planet, the moon in the Arctic shows the changing face of his waxing and waning. But during the winter, when the moon is full, it does not rise and set as it does further south. Because a full moon occurs when the sun is opposite the moon, if the sun does not appear in the sky at all the moon does not disappear. It just travels round and round the horizon. But as the moon wanes, and becomes a new moon, for days there will be no light in the sky other than starlight.

Some Inuit people tell the story of how the moon chases his sister, the sun, who was unmarried and lived alone. He came to her alone in her igloo, and the lamps went out; in

the darkness he raped her, and then he left her. When he returned on the next night, she dipped her finger in the bottom of the lamp, where the soot collects, and when he raped her again she brushed her hand on his face, marking him with the soot. Then she went looking for the man who had done this, and found it was her brother. In their shame, they do not appear in the sky at the same time, and the soot marks on his face are the shadows we see on the face of the moon at night.

The return of the sun in the spring is the most important

Sea ice covers the surface of the Arctic and Antarctic oceans

event in the year. The new, fragile sun is welcomed by songs and ceremonies and, so as not to offend her, all the lamps are extinguished so that she has no rivals. And when the sun returns so do other visitors to the Arctic.

Many creatures make the long, arduous journey north on migrations that bring them thousands of kilometres. They come here for the sunlight, for the long days. Grey whales spend their winters in the waters off Baja California, where they give birth to their calves, then swim northwards, along the Pacific coast of North America, to spend

summer in the Arctic waters. Here, they feed on shrimps and molluscs in the mud. They lie on their sides, scooping up mud and filtering through baleen plates in their mouths, making distinctive 'feeding furrows' in the seabed. The adults and their calves feed all summer, putting on fat. In the same way, humpback whales make their journeys from the tropical waters of the Atlantic or the Pacific and spend their summer in the north, feeding on tiny fish like capelin.

The few brief months of summer bring an explosion of life to the Arctic. In a ferment of colour, plants burst into flower, completing their cycle in a matter of weeks. And wave upon wave of insects emerge – midges and mosquitoes. So the birds that fly here from their wintering grounds have two bonuses: the long days, when they can spend most of their time feeding, and as much food as they can eat. The shallow pools, formed by the snow melting over the permafrost, are crowded with ducks, geese and swans, who have all flown north to breed and raise a family. Many of these birds have an unfailing ability to navigate; they return to the same sites each year, often after a journey of more than 1,000 km (620 miles).

In the Arctic regions of Canada, snow geese return to the same nest site they left the previous year. They brave the occasional late storm to make all they can of the light. And as the chicks are hatched, like all the young wildfowl, they must put on bodyweight as fast as they can. They will need to be strong enough at the end of the summer to follow their parents on the return journey south. At the same time as the chicks are eating and growing, their parents are moulting the worn flight feathers that brought them all the way to the Arctic, replacing them with new ones before the next long flight.

All too soon, winter will begin its relentless approach. There is a fine balance between staying as long as possible to gain strength and leaving before being caught by the first bad weather of winter. But, inevitably, they must leave. Young cygnets will be almost as big as their parents, but will still have the patchy brown of their juvenile feathers. All the young birds must be ready to follow their parents on the journey. It will be the hardest trial of their lives.

But not all the birds leave. Around Lake Myvatn, in Iceland, some of the whooper swans stay all winter. The geothermal activity under the surface keeps some of the pools from freezing, and the Gulf Stream brushing Iceland creates milder winters than other places this far north. Why some swans decide to stay and others decide to leave is a mystery, but the ones who are setting out on the long journey south do so before winter arrives. These families of whooper swans fly through the night, making a continuous flight of 1,100 km (700 miles) without a break, taking as long as 15 hours to do so. They are heading for wintering grounds further south, some to Scotland, some to the

A grey whale feeds by scooping up mud from the sea floor and filtering it through baleen plates

Washes in the southeast of England. Geese fly fast and high; the barheaded goose even migrates over the Himalayas, reaching heights of 9,000 m (30,000 ft). They fly in skeins, so that they can take turns either flying in the lead or in the slipstream of the bird ahead, forming the recognizable V-shape as they pass overhead.

Some birds manage to bask in summer all year. Arctic terns spend the summer in the Arctic, but when winter approaches they leave and fly all the way to Antarctica, which is emerging into summer as the Arctic descends into winter. They make this journey of 16,000 km (10,000 miles) twice a year, the longest flights of any migrating birds.

There are no land mammals on the huge continent of Antarctica. Twice the size of Australia, Antarctica was the 'Terra Australis Incognita', the mysterious landmass hinted at on ancient maps, but unknown to Europeans until it was discovered by James Cook in 1773. Ninety-eight per cent of the continent is covered by a massive icesheet, up to 4 km (2½ miles) thick in places, making it the highest of the continents. The weight of all this ice pushes the land itself down below sea level, and at its base some of this ice could

Whooper swans return to the Arctic each year to raise their families

be more than 200,000 years old. Yet there was a time when this land was not dominated by the ice. Fossils of ferns and deposits of coal suggest that the climate was almost tropical 70 million years ago; the land that would become Antarctica must have started out near the equator and drifted south. Ammonite fossils also hint that the seas round the continent were once warm, but Antarctica now is the coldest place on the planet.

Like the Arctic, it has long cold winters and brief summers. The cold water round the coast is very fertile and teeming with sea life. But because the water is so cold, marine animals grow more slowly, and produce fewer and larger eggs than their counterparts in warmer waters. And growing more slowly they live longer; some sponges are known to be hundreds of years old. They also grow bigger. A bizarre creature, *Glyptonotus antarcticus*, which lives on the seabed, is a relative of the common woodlouse – except that it grows up to 20 cm (8 in) long.

In addition, also as in the Arctic, birds and whales migrate here for the summer to gorge themselves on the thriving sea life. Of all the birds, penguins are the best adapted to the cold, and although they cannot fly and seem inelegant on land, they are masters of the water. But the emperor penguin, standing up to 1.2 m (4 ft) in height, is the only penguin that will stay on Antarctica when winter comes, the male and female taking turns to incubate the egg in the cold and dark while the other goes off to feed. They huddle in large groups to keep warm, also taking turns to stand on the outside of the group, shielding the others from the wind.

It very rarely snows in the interior of Antarctica, although the violent, turbulent winds can whip up the dry ice crystals into a 'blizzard', even though the skies above may be clear. And the main problem for humans who live and work on the continent is the wind chill. Fierce storms circulate round the continent as the cold, dry, polar air clashes with the moist, warmer air over the southern Atlantic, Indian and Pacific Oceans; gusts of more than 160 kph (100 mph) are not uncommon.

But despite its harsh, bleak conditions, Antarctica draws people to its icy wastes. In the nineteenth century, ships came here on great seal-hunting expeditions, and drove the seals close to extinction. In the beginning of the twentieth century, exploration of the interior began; the South Pole was reached in 1911 by the Norwegian, Roald Amundsen, who arrived a month ahead of the British expedition led by Robert Scott. All Scott's men died on the return from the pole, but the cold, dry air has preserved their living quarters, now left as a monument to their heroism.

Antarctica is now a shared land; seven nations decreed sovereignty over the continent in the first decades of the twentieth century, although since the Antarctic Treaty of 1961 these are no longer enforced, and Antarctica remains the last place on the planet where the spirit of international cooperation and scientific research overrides national boundaries and territorial claims.

Snow

Snow comes in many shapes and forms, depending on the temperature and amount of water vapour in the atmosphere. Snow is not frozen rain, although rain is sometimes melted snow; the difference is in the formation of the crystals that make up snowflakes.

The crucial temperature is −40°C (−40°F). Above this, water vapour in the air needs a nucleus to crystallize onto, in the same way that a raindrop forms around a condensation nucleus. Below this temperature, water vapour can crystallize out as tiny ice crystals, without a nucleus.

The life of a snowflake begins with the formation of ice crystals that are usually hexagonal in shape, and often beautifully intricate. If the temperature is very low, and there is little water vapour in the air, the crystals stay small, and if they fall, they fall as dry, powdery snow. If the temperature is nearer 0°C (32°F), the crystals tend to stick together around a nucleus, melting slightly and forming big flakes.

If the snow or ice crystals stay small and light, they exist as a cloud in the middle or upper layers of the atmosphere. But when the snowflakes are heavy enough they fall to the ground. As they fall they melt, and if the air through which they fall is warmer than the cloud the snowflakes turn into rain. But the process of melting cools the air around it, so it may stay cold enough for the snowflake to refreeze. The ideal temperature for snow is around 0°C (32°F), as the warmer the snow, the more moisture it contains, so the snowflakes are large and heavy enough to fall to the ground.

If very cold air lies at ground level, and a layer of warmer air sits above it, the water vapour in the cold air crystallizes at the boundary, and the tiny ice crystals float to the ground, glittering as they do. This is *diamond dust,* and can occur even when there are no clouds in the sky. When tiny ice crystals form like this in the sky, they can produce optical illusions, such as haloes round the sun.

When the snow falls to the ground, whether or not it will settle depends on the wind, as well as the temperature and humidity. Dry, cold, powdery snow remains loose on the ground, and provides excellent skiing. Wet snow that melts and reforms as ice gets harder, and if more snow falls on top of it, it becomes compacted. In polar

Close-up of a snow crystal

areas, if the snow does not melt each year and more snow accumulates, eventually the underlying ice forms a glacier.

In mountainous regions, if loose snow falls onto an underlying hard layer, there is the danger of an avalanche. This can also occur if the temperature changes so that the snow crystals do not stick together as readily; when this happens the layer of snow becomes unstable, and may slide downhill at the slightest trigger.

The Great Cycle

chapter 14

Unite and Unite and Let us all Unite

For summer is acome unto Day

And Whither we are going, we will all Unite

In the Merry Morning of May.

Padstow May song

To our ancestors, the ability to understand and predict the changes in the seasons meant the difference between life and death. It was that important. Even the first hunter-gatherer tribes had to understand the seasonal movements of the herds, and know when the different plants would appear. For the societies that lived by planting and harvesting, it was even more crucial to know when to sow and when to reap. It was a question of predicting the changes in the seasons, to plant so that the first shoots appeared at a certain time, to harvest before the winter storms destroyed the crops that were so essential for survival. So the need to anticipate changes in the seasons was more than just marking the passage of time.

Of the ancient, huge megalithic structures which act as massive calendars, the greatest is Stonehenge, situated on England's Salisbury Plain. Built more than 4,000 years ago,

The sun rises over Stonehenge, England, on midsummer morning

***Overleaf:** The shadow of a serpent moves down the steps of the Castillo at Chichen Itza on the Spring Equinox*

its meaning and purpose is lost in prehistory. But for someone standing at the centre of the main ring of stones, the sarsen circle, on midsummer morning, the sun rises behind the Heel Stone, a solitary stone over 75 m (250 ft) away. There is an academic discussion about whether the monument was designed to predict more complex alignments, but there is no doubt that this massive temple was a major religious centre for centuries. Even now, people are drawn to the stones on the summer solstice to watch the sun rise, as did the mysterious builders of Stonehenge thousands of years ago.

Furthermore, there is no doubt that these huge monuments, which marked the turning points of the year, are powerful religious symbols that still have a hold on us. In Mexico, the Mayan temple complex of Chichen Itza is not as old as Stonehenge, but it draws people with the same fascination. On 21 March, the spring equinox, more than 45,000 people make the pilgrimage to the ancient site to watch the feathered serpent, Kukulcan, appear on the steps of the main temple, the square pyramid known as the *Castillo*.

Stonehenge

There is more speculation and fantasy written about the great, imposing, mysterious stones of Stonehenge than there is agreed, factual information. They have stood like sentinels on England's Salisbury Plain since before history began, and there have been many and varied theories about their origins. But no one really knows why they were raised, what purpose this monument served.

It was once suggested that Stonehenge was raised by the Druids, but the Druids were Celtic priests and the first phase of building was thought to have started around 2900 BC – which is 2,000 years before the Celts came to Britain. The first structure at the site was a circular ditch nearly 100 m (330 ft) in diameter, about 6 m (20 ft) wide and 2 m (6 ft) deep, with earth banks either side of the ditch. Two stones were placed at the entrance to the circle, and one survives, although it has since fallen over. It is now known as the Slaughter Stone. Fifty-six holes were also dug at this period, although later filled in; these were discovered by John Aubrey in the seventeenth century and named the Aubrey Holes after him.

The second phase of building started about 2500 BC, when timber posts were used. All that remains of them now are the filled-in holes they once occupied. Then, from 2500 to 1600 BC, the third phase saw the addition of the famous stone monoliths

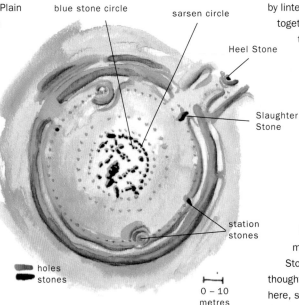

blue stone circle
sarsen circle
Heel Stone
Slaughter Stone
station stones
holes
stones
0 – 10 metres

Layout of Stonehenge

which were brought to the area, probably from the Preseli Mountains in Wales. These first stones, the blue stones, were the smallest, at about 2 m (6 ft) high, and were stood in two concentric circles. The process of building Stonehenge seems to have been a continuous one, because at some point

these circles were dismantled. Huge blocks of sarsen stone were brought from the Marlborough Downs to create the next phase.

When stood upright, these stones were 4 m (13 ft) high. The sarsen stones were used to create a circle, with the uprights crowned by lintels of the same stone, all fitting together, all forming a continuous ring. The top of this circle was exactly horizontal, even though the ground is slightly sloping. Inside this ring, a horseshoe shape was made of sarsen stones. The other stones that are still there – the Slaughter Stone, the Altar Stone and the Heel Stone – are not accurately dated, so it is uncertain at which point they were added.

The Heel Stone stands some distance outside the stone circle, but from the centre of the ring the midsummer sun rises behind the Heel Stone on the summer solstice. It is thought that originally there were two stones here, so that the sun rose between them. The summer solstice still draws people to Stonehenge, even though its original purpose has been lost with the passing of time. Stonehenge was probably built as a temple, and possibly an ancient form of calendar, but whatever rituals were performed here thousands of years ago the ancient stones still inspire a sense of mystery and awe.

In the late afternoon, the sun's rays catch the steps of the northwestern corner of the pyramid and create a rippled, zigzag shadow down the central staircase. It looks very much like a diamondback rattlesnake, with the carved serpent's head at the base completing the image. The serpent, particularly the feathered serpent, is a powerful symbol; he brings the life-giving power of the sky – the rain and sun – down to Earth. Serpents were also connected to the passage of time, the cycle of the year, birth, death and renewal. Again, it is not certain whether the pyramid was originally designed to create this image at the spring equinox, but the effect of the shadow meeting the carved stone serpent's head makes it likely that this was the case.

Throughout the world, the sun and moon were wor-shipped as deities. The sun had the power of life and death, and was itself seen to die and be born again as the year turned, in the same way as the moon died and was reborn every month. So the changes in the sun's strength and power formed the basis for marking the passage of the year. Although our ancestors did not understand the mechanisms that generated the solstices and equinoxes, they built their religions around these crucial events of the year.

Whereas many ancient peoples marked the passing of the solstices and equinoxes, we have inherited our main festivals from the calendar of a people who dominated Europe for many centuries – the Celts. For the Celts, the important stations of the year were the four festivals that fell halfway between the equinox and solstice points. These were the 'cross-quarter days', and we still celebrate them in one form or another today.

The first cross-quarter day of the year is *Imbolc*, halfway between the winter solstice and the spring equinox, so it occurs around 1 February. *Imbolc* means 'time of ewe's milk', referring to the first appearance of newborn lambs in the fields. It is the first glimmer of the onset of spring, when the early flowers bloom on the forest floor. They appear before the trees regrow their leaves and the canopy blocks the sunlight. The Christian Church celebrates this time as *Candlemas*, by lighting candles. It commemorates the time when the Virgin Mary presented the young Jesus to the Temple, 40 days after his birth, but it has been mainly a celebration of the Virgin Mary herself. It is also the feast day of St Brigit, the ancient goddess of poetry and the arts, an aspect of the threefold goddess of Celtic religion, who was taken into Christianity and canonized.

In America, the tradition of Groundhog Day, 2 February, celebrates the time when the groundhog, or woodchuck, comes out from hibernation to look for his shadow. If he sees it, it is an omen of six more weeks of bad weather, so he goes back into his hole; if the day is cloudy there is no shadow, spring is on its way and he stays out. The tradition comes from an ancient English song:

> *If Candlemas be fair and bright, Come Winter, have*
> *another flight.*
> *If Candlemas brings cloud and rain, Go Winter, and*
> *come not again.*

Spring has arrived by the time Easter is celebrated. It has its origins in the festival of Eastre, the Anglo-Saxon goddess of fertility. Her consort was the hare, a powerful symbol of fertility, and as the festival was taken over by Christianity this pagan symbol was transformed into a rabbit, the Easter bunny. Eggs are an obvious fertility symbol, and the practices of giving eggs as gifts, painting them in bright colours and playing egg-rolling games derive from Eastre's festival.

The thorny question of the date of Easter has a complicated origin in the history of the Church. The earlier pagan versions of the festival were celebrated at the spring equinox in March. Early Christians celebrated the Resurrection immediately after the festival of Passover, which was originally calculated by the Babylonian calendar, a calendar based on the moon's phases. Easter is calculated to fall on the first Sunday after the full moon that follows the spring equinox, but if this coincides with the festival of Passover it

is celebrated on the Sunday afterwards. Hence Easter can fall anywhere between 22 March and 25 April. And Easter is now the only date of a major festival that is still calculated by the positions of the moon and sun.

In Europe, people celebrate *May Day*, now marked on 1 May; this is a relic of the ancient festival of Beltane, occurring halfway between the spring equinox, 21 March, and the summer solstice, 21 June. It was a great festival of fertility, the first day of summer, and, like many of the Celtic festivals, was the time to light great bonfires, the 'Beltane Fire', to welcome the summer sun. But the early Celtic festivals were not limited to one day or one night. They lasted for several days and were probably celebrated at the nearest full moon. It was a time for feasting and dancing, when couples made love under the moonlight; a child conceived at the Beltane fires was believed to be a child of the ancient goddess of fertility, and the father had no claim to its paternity.

The relic of the fertility symbolism is still found when the maypole is raised and decorated with ribbons; young children dance around the maypole, entwining their ribbons to make colourful patterns. In Bavaria, the celebration involves a whole village erecting a huge maypole, and couples dance around the pole in pairs. At the same time, horses are decorated with flowers, which are woven into their bridles, manes and tail. This is possibly an ancient link to the worship of the horse goddess, Epona, from whom we get our word 'pony'.

Gathering in the harvest at the end of the summer – the sun-ripened corn was a gift from the Earth

In late summer, between the summer solstice and the autumn equinox, the festival of *Lughnasah*, a lesser festival now, was dedicated to the sun-god, Lugh. It is also known as *Lammas*, and is celebrated on 1 August. It was the beginning of the harvest, when the first corn was ripening, and the first bread was baked with the new corn. The harvest was always more than just a practical event, it was the time to give thanks for the successful gathering of the crops; today, the Harvest Festival is very much a part of the Church year. But in the days when the corn was a gift from the Earth, from the mother goddess in her different guises, the spirit of the corn had to be honoured. At the end of the harvest, when all the crops were safely gathered in, the stalks of the last corn cut were used to make a cage, a home to keep the spirit of the fields safe until the following spring. These *corn dollies* were often made with exquisite workmanship, and their connection with the fertility of the Earth turned them into fertility symbols in their own right.

Later into autumn, as the days became shorter and the nights were long and cold, came the best-known of the Celtic festivals, thought to be the start of their new year. This was the great feast of *Samhain* (pronounced 'Sowan'). It marked the start of winter; the sun was getting weaker, and again bonfires were lit to give strength to the dying sun. It brought the onset of darkness and chaos, and the veils between the physical world and the spiritual world became thinner, so the souls of the dead could come back to Earth. We know this festival as 'Hallowe'en'.

Across North America, Hallowe'en has become an occasion for ghouls and ghosts and witches, with pumpkin masks, parties and the tradition of 'trick or treat'. In Europe, in the twentieth century, the ancient festival has evolved into a similar round of parties with themes of ghosts and witches. The Celtic festival was transformed into a superstitious acknowledgement of the dark side of the spirit world by the Church. For the Celts, a day ran from sunset to

Padstow on Mayday

The town of Padstow, in Cornwall, England, is the focus of a celebration of the coming of spring, the first day of May, that draws visitors from far and wide. The traditional greeting of the summer is a festival that involves the whole town.

As with many of the Mayday festivals, the streets are decked out with greenery and colourful flags and bunting. But the main ceremony centres around two 'Obby 'Osses, that weave their way round separate routes through the town, only coming together in the evening.

The term 'Obby 'Oss is a corruption of 'hobby horse', and 'hobby' comes from the fourteenth-century word for a small horse. A circular frame, nearly 2 m (6 ft) across is worn by the person playing the 'Obby 'Oss; it is hung from the shoulders, covered in black oilskin with a black oilskin 'skirt' that hangs down from the frame. On the front of the frame is a carved horse's head, and on the back a tail of horsehair, and the operator wears a painted grotesque mask.

In the festival, the 'Oss is led by a dancer, the 'Teaser', who dances in front of the 'Oss, waving a club, a shield-shaped bat with a handle. The Teaser's purpose is to keep the 'Oss dancing and following, swinging the frame and skirt as it does. Crowds line the route, and the 'Oss is followed by a retinue of 'Mayers' – those celebrating May – who are dressed in white. One 'Oss , the Old 'Oss, has followers who wear red ribbons and sashes on their white garments, and the other 'Oss, the Blue 'Oss, has followers who wear blue ribbons and sashes on their white garments. Occasionally the 'Oss makes a lunge at a young woman in the crowd; he covers her with the skirt, which means she will have a baby – or find a husband – in the following year.

Everyone sings the May Songs, accompanied by musicians playing accordions and drums, as the two processions dance through the streets. Then, every now and again, the pace changes, the song becomes a dirge, and the 'Oss 'dies', sinking to the ground. Then the Teaser strokes the 'Oss with the club, and as the music gathers pace again the 'Oss springs back to life, and the procession continues.

There is much speculation about the origins of this festival, and it does draw on traditions seen elsewhere in England at Mayday. It has been suggested that it is an ancient pagan celebration of the fertility of spring, but it seems that the first recorded description of the festival was as late as 1803. The Padstow ceremony has grown in response to the interest and enthusiasm shown by visitors as well as the town people themselves. But the singing, the prancing of the 'Obby 'Osses, the dancing and the colours are nevertheless a powerful invocation of spring and all that it brings.

Padstow May Day celebrations

sunset, so Samhain, would run from the night of 31 October until sunset on 1 November. In a bid to eliminate the ancient pagan festivals, the Church declared two feast days; 1 November became 'All Saints Day' or 'All Hallows Day', and so the night before, 31 October, became 'All Hallows Eve' – Hallowe'en. But the old traditions do not die that easily.

In England, the date has maintained a bizarre link with the fire festival of Samhain. It is no coincidence that the anniversary of one of history's spectacular failures has been turned into a major bonfire and firework festival at the beginning of November, the same time of year as Samhain. The attempts of a certain Guy Fawkes and his accomplices to blow up the Houses of Parliament, in 1605, met in failure as they were discovered and arrested.

When King James I succeeded the Protestant Elizabeth I, he promised to be more tolerant of the country's Catholics, who had been persecuted for decades under Elizabeth, and before that under her father, Henry VIII. But James was a weak, unpopular king, and, when it became obvious that nothing much would change, a plot was hatched to blow up the House of Lords when the King was there for the Opening of Parliament. The group of 13 conspirators included Guy Fawkes, an explosives expert. But the group was betrayed, and as Guy Fawkes was preparing the explosives and fuses on the night of 4 November, in the cellar under the House of Lords, he was discovered and arrested. Under gruesome torture he revealed the names of the other traitors and he was tried and executed by being hanged, drawn and quartered. Parliament ordained that 5 November be a day of Thanksgiving for their escape. But 'Guy Fawkes Night', of 5 November, with its effigies of Fawkes being burned on a bonfire and the letting-off of fireworks, still touches a distant memory of the greatest festival of the year, the fire festival of Samhain.

Which brings us to the last and the greatest festival of the year, now celebrated all over the world. Christmas. There is no historical evidence to show that Christ was born

At the end of the year, we celebrate Christmas, a festival of warmth and light

on 25 December, and the current date for Christmas was not set until around AD 300. Christian thinkers of the third century believed that the world was created at the spring equinox, which was then thought to fall on 25 March. This was when Christ was incarnated, or conceived, so his birth would be nine months later on 25 December. But long before then the winter solstice was celebrated, the turning point in the year when the sun began to recover its strength. It is probable that the Church also set the day as a way of taking control of the many pagan celebrations of the rebirth of the sun, including the Roman festival which marked the birth of the 'unconquered sun'.

The traditions we associate with Christmas today have many and varied origins. The parties and exchanges of gifts came from another Roman festival, that of Saturnalia, and the decorating of evergreen trees, the Yule log and Yule cake are relics of the Germanic celebration of Yule, again at the winter solstice. It is thought that the familiar figure of Santa Claus originated from the Dutch festival of St Nicholas, also known as Sinterklaas (a derivation of Sink Niklaas) – or Santa Claus. He visited children, bringing them gifts if they had behaved themselves, in preparation for the arrival of the Christ child.

The Dutch took the tradition to America when they formed their colony of New Amsterdam, now New York, and British settlers took over the tradition as part of their Christmas Eve celebrations. However, the exchange of greetings cards is a more recent tradition which began only in the nineteenth century.

Living in cities, we are not so finely tuned to the passing of the seasons and the turning of the year as were our ancestors. When they learned to conquer and control fire, they could bring the light and warmth of the sun down to Earth, so we are now free from the tyranny of winter. We still celebrate the festivals of the year without realizing their original connections to the turning of the seasons, but they do not lose their popularity. They give us a structure to time, to the great cycle of the year.

PART FOUR
GAIA'S CHILDREN

The Gaia Hypothesis

chapter 15

I think one of the great exciting science adventures of the

last twenty years has been the so-called Gaia

Hypothesis...because what it's done is to inspire a debate

about the notion of inter-connectedness, of the whole planet,

of the planet as an organism.

Jonathan Porritt

When we first left the security of our safe, solid world to venture into space, it would change our view of the planet for ever. We watched through the eyes of the astronauts, as they gazed down on the Earth, and shared the profound experience this gave them. Cosmonaut Aleksei Leonov described it:

The Earth was small, light blue, and so touchingly alone, our home that must be defended like a holy relic. The Earth was absolutely round. I believe I never knew what the word 'round' meant until I saw Earth from space.

The images that the space age generated inspired new perceptions of the Earth, not as the local neighbourhood in which we live, or the country, or even the continent, but as

a fragile, blue and white jewel, and *this* is all we have.

It was in the late 1960s that new ways of seeing the Earth were formed. James Lovelock, an English scientist working at the Jet Propulsion Laboratory in Pasadena, was involved in the planning of expeditions to Mars, and was asked to help with ways of investigating whether there could be life on Mars. As he considered the conditions needed for life and the differences between Mars and Earth, he realized that there was a way of considering the Earth that would allow a different approach to understanding it.

Why has the Earth been *such* a suitable place for life for most of its long history? The planet has been through many changes in its history, including being hit by massive meteors, many miles across; huge volcanic eruptions, dramatic changes in climate and continents that drift around. And the sun, that sustains life on Earth, has also changed, getting hotter as it burns.

But, however much conditions changed, they never changed beyond that needed to sustain life. Lovelock suggested that, although life adapts to the changing circumstances around it, life also creates changes of its own. We have already seen how a form of life, cyanobacteria, created the oxygen in the atmosphere and changed the planet for ever. So life can affect the conditions across the whole planet. But is it possible that life and the planet could actually be part of the same system? That the Earth could regulate and adjust itself in the same way that a living organism does?

This concept – of the Earth as a single, self-regulating organism – was given a name, 'Gaia', after the Greek goddess of the Earth. Lovelock was working with biologist Lynn Margulis, who worked on microbes and the way they changed their surroundings. And it turned out that microbes, the smallest creatures on the planet, are in fact capable of making the biggest changes. Even though we cannot see them, they exist in such huge numbers that they can affect the whole planet. One possible way that life could change conditions on the Earth involves tiny *Coccolithophores*, a form of plankton living in the oceans. They have shells made of chalk – calcium carbonate – and they make these shells by absorbing carbon dioxide.

When they die, they sink to the bottom of the ocean, taking carbon dioxide out of the atmosphere. But if the Earth became warmer it is possible that *Coccolithophores* would breed more rapidly and absorb more carbon dioxide. As carbon dioxide is a greenhouse gas, it keeps the planet relatively warm. If the amount of carbon dioxide was reduced, the planet would cool down. In other words, these plankton could, in theory, regulate the temperature of the Earth.

Like many new, radical ideas, the Gaia hypothesis was vehemently rejected by many scientists. Criticism of the

The space programme gave humans a unique view of our home world

Gaia hypothesis came from several directions, but in each case it inspired Lovelock and Margulis to refine the theory in order to answer their critics. One of the criticisms was that the Earth is essentially a lump of rock with a thin veneer of life on the surface, so how could it be alive? In response, American physicist Jerome Rothstein proposed the analogy of a redwood tree. These giant trees, the largest living things on the planet, consist of a central core of dead wood. Around the outside, the bark that protects the tree is also dead; the living part of the tree is the thin layer under the bark, the *cambium*, the layers of cells that grow and reproduce. The leaves on the branches and the living cambium layer, in total, add up to 3 per cent of the tree; the rest is dead, inert. In the same way, the Earth has a dead interior, is covered by a layer of life and on top of that, the inert atmosphere protects that layer of life from the radiation of space.

Another major criticism argued that, in order for the Earth to be considered a living organism, like any other organism it must have somehow evolved. But evolution occurs over generations through small changes as organisms reproduce. The critics against Gaia say the Earth could not reproduce, and so therefore it could not evolve into a self-regulating organism. Another challenge to the idea was that, for life to change the planet, individuals would have to cooperate, and to cooperate they would need to communicate. As the major changes are made by the small life forms, there would need to be global communication between them, which is unlikely to say the least.

But Lovelock is a chemist and inventor; to defend his idea he proposed an example that would be self-regulating, but would not involve cooperation or purpose, or the need for the system slowly to evolve. He described an imaginary planet, orbiting a sun very similar to ours, that grows hotter as it burns. This planet is covered in daisies, so it is named 'Daisyworld', and in Lovelock's first model the daisies were either white or black.

The daisies grow best at a temperature of 22.5°C (73°F), but can survive within a range of, say, 5–40°C (40–100°F). As the sun burns, it eventually warms up enough so that, on the imaginary planet, the temperature reaches 5°C (40°F) at the equator, and the first daisies can germinate. Life begins with a few daisies growing round the equator; initially a mixture of black and white daisies germinate. But as it is still cool, the black daisies do better than the white ones. Black daisies absorb heat from the sun, and themselves get warm, and as they do they radiate the heat and so warm their surroundings. White daisies reflect heat, like snow, and so stay cool, and cool their surroundings. The bare ground is neutral.

Black daisies do better at the beginning, when the temperature is cool, as they can absorb heat and keep warm, whereas the white daisies do not do so well. There are more black daisies, so they spread their seeds and flourish. They retain the sun's heat at the surface, thus warming the planet more than the bare ground. The planet is now warmer than it would be with just the heat from the sun.

Gaia – a new view of the Earth

But the sun is still getting hotter, so the combination of dark daisies and warm sun eventually pushes up the temperature. The few white daisies around now do better, as the temperature approaches the 22.5°C (73°F) that is the ideal temperature for both kinds of daisies. There is now an even mixture of daisies over the planet.

However, the sun's heat is still increasing, so at Daisyworld's equator it starts to get even warmer. Now the white daisies do better than the black daisies as they reflect the heat and keep cool. So white daisies start to spread from the equator, and when there are mostly white daisies they keep the planet cooler than it would be if it was just bare ground. Throughout the period of growth of the daisies, the temperature of the planet has been kept within a narrow range, ideal for daisies, even though the heat from the sun is increasing.

Eventually, the sun's heat will increase to a point where even the white daisies cannot cool down enough, so, starting at the equator, the daisies will die, leaving behind bare ground, the desert. Now, without the daisies, there is nothing to cool the planet, so it quickly reaches the temperature it would have been if left unchecked, and the daisies all die. Daisyworld is now dead.

This imaginary world of daisies may seem to be idle speculation, an interesting theory. But it is the fundamental basis for the Gaia hypothesis, as it shows that life can regulate a planet without any communication; the daisies do not talk to each other, they are simply responding to their surroundings. There is no long-term purpose, the planet is not acting with any intent or will, yet the overall effect is to keep the temperature constant even though the sun is getting hotter. It does not last for ever; like any living organism, the planet eventually dies, but while the daisies are living the planet acts *like* a living organism, self-regulating, self-adjusting.

Planet Earth, is, of course, much more complicated than Daisyworld. The first Daisyworld concept was a system that could be described by mathematical equations and modelled on a computer, so that the growth and decay of the daisies and their effect on the planet could be simulated. Lovelock expanded the model, adding in grey daisies. This was to answer the critics who suggested that because grey daisies did not need to use energy in making pigment, they would flourish because they could 'cheat' and not do any

Giant redwood trees – the living cells under the bark surround a core of dead wood

The Birth of Gaia

Dr James Lovelock came up with his revolutionary idea in the 1960s:

I was working at the Jet Propulsion Laboratory in California; the great topic in those days was – is there life on Mars? This was the great inspiration that kept Americans going and produced money for space research. My job was really as an instrument designer, but I couldn't help being curious about the experiments my biological colleagues were proposing to send to Mars. Most of them looked to me a bit absurd. They were mostly to send an automated laboratory there to pick up bits of soil and look at it, and see if there were organisms that would grow on culture plates.

When you asked them what they used in their culture plates, you found they used the same things that they used on Earth. So they were expecting to find Earth-type

organisms living on Mars. I thought this had a very poor chance of success. The spacecraft might land somewhere like an icecap, where there wasn't any life; you wouldn't find life on Earth if it landed on Antarctica.

I thought maybe there's a better way of doing it. If you analysed the atmosphere of the whole planet, instead of just looking at the surface, if there was life there you would find it would be obliged to use the atmosphere as a source of its raw materials. And also as a place to deposit its waste products. That would change the composition of the atmosphere in a way that would make it recognizably different from a planet that didn't have life on it. The planet that was barren and lifeless would be very close to what's called a chemical equilibrium state, which is well known and almost predictable.

And in the course of time we found that Mars was very close to the equilibrium state, and according to the theory had no life on it. This was confirmed by the Viking

spacecraft which landed there in 1976.

But looking at Mars this way forced one to look back at the Earth as the control planet. This was a planet that did have life, so was its atmosphere in disequilibrium? The answer was, it wasn't just in disequilibrium, it was extraordinarily in disequilibrium.

You have extraordinary things like oxygen and methane mixed in the air, and they're reactive. If the composition were different, it would be an explosive mixture. Yet those gases stay steady at a constant concentration all the time. And one of them, oxygen, is just at the right level for life.

Now this seemed to be too much for me, and I thought there must be something on the Earth that's regulating them.

He had realized that life itself was regulating the atmosphere, that the planet and the life on it could be thought of as a single, self-regulating organism. He called the idea Gaia, after the Greek goddess of the Earth.

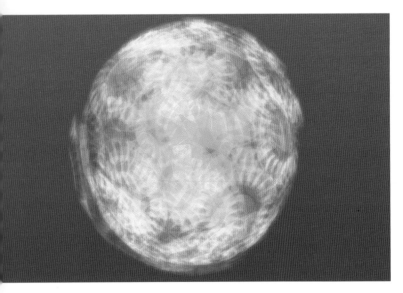

Coccolithophore, microscopic ocean plankton

But hydrogen sulphide breaks down quickly in water containing oxygen, such as seawater. Lovelock was not convinced. However, there is a chemical, which goes by the name of *dimethyl sulphide*, or the more manageable DMS; it also partly consists of sulphur. He knew from the work of other scientists that algae, the microscopic creatures of the ocean, emitted DMS as a waste product.

Maybe this was the way that sulphur was returned to the land, through the action of plankton in the oceans. Lovelock went on an expedition on the RV *Shackleton*, sailing from the UK to Antarctica in 1972, and with some basic scientific equipment found the presence of DMS and another gas, carbon sulphide; it seemed evident that he had solved the sulphur puzzle. But this was not a particularly dramatic conclusion, other than that land animals would not run out

work. But when Lovelock ran the model including the grey daisies he still found the black daisies did best when it was too cold, and the white daisies when it was too hot; even if he allowed for the black and white daisies using up some of their energy making pigments, the model still produced the same result.

But is the Earth really like a computer game with flowers? On the Earth, there are similarities with Daisyworld. Like the daisies, ocean plankton such as *Coccolithophores* may be capable of regulating the temperature by changing the levels of carbon dioxide in the atmosphere. And our sun, an average star like any other star, has been getting hotter as it burns; it is something like 30 per cent hotter now than when it first formed. Yet it seems that the average temperature of the Earth has stayed within certain limits since life appeared.

Another way in which regulation could occur was discovered in 1971. Lovelock was interested in the element sulphur, an element needed by creatures living on the land. But sulphur is washed away from the land, as rainwater flows into rivers which flow into the sea, carrying sulphur in solution with it. But, clearly, the land was not running out of sulphur, so there must be some way of it being recycled, replenishing the land.

It had been assumed by scientists that the puzzle was solved by the gas hydrogen sulphide being emitted by the oceans into the atmosphere. It would be carried by rain, so replenishing the land. Anyone who has had an uncomfortably close contact with rotten eggs will be familiar with the smell of hydrogen sulphide, so it should be easy to detect.

of sulphur. So what has this got to do with the weather?

The meteorologists Robert Charleson and Stephen Warren suggested that the emission of DMS from algae in the ocean might be crucial for the formation of clouds in the atmosphere. We saw in Chapter 5 that water droplets do not just condense out of nowhere, they must have something to condense *onto*. They realized that, as the DMS broke down in the atmosphere, it formed tiny droplets that would be the nuclei for the water vapour to condense, and hence form clouds.

But white clouds reflect sunlight back into space, so the more cloud there is the cooler the Earth will be. If the production of DMS is affected by temperature, say if the warmer it was the more DMS was produced, then there would be more cloud – and the Earth would cool down.

Like the black and white daisies, the algae would be controlling the temperature of the planet.

Not enough is known about this process to draw a definite conclusion, and Lovelock's Gaia hypothesis has not been conclusively proved or disproved. But, if nothing else, it has started people thinking in a different way and started people asking different questions about the planet. It is making us realize that the connections between things are as important – or more important – than the things themselves. The idea seems to have caught the popular imagination; it has made people aware that small changes in the Earth's conditions could have consequences for the whole planet.

Clouds form on condensation nuclei and reflect sunlight back into space

Watering the Desert

chapter 16

Water flows uphill to money.

The Dammed – *Fred Pearce*

Las Vegas – the ultimate playground. Built out of nothing, in the desert of Nevada, it has become a symbol of our ability to tame the wilderness. The city is only 100 years old, and is built on an oasis; the first European to find this oasis was Rafael Rivera in the eighteenth century. It was marked on the maps as 'Vegas', meaning 'Meadows', referring to grassland alongside the streams that had formed by upwelling springs, bringing water from underground, where it seeps down from the mountains that lie to the west.

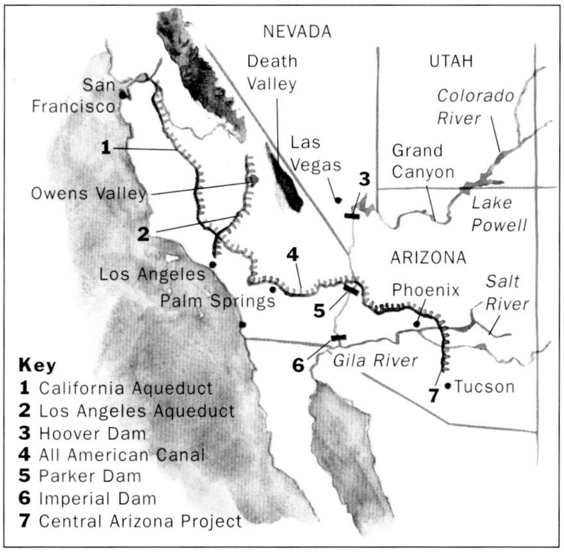

Sometime at the beginning of the nineteenth century, the name was changed to Las Vegas, and by the middle of the century the Mormons had created a settlement. In 1864 a fort was built, Fort Baker, to protect the route through to California, but by the 1890s the railroad developers realized that this would make a prime stop-over point and the town was born.

Saloons, stores, and boarding houses sprang up almost

Fountain Hills, Phoenix, Arizona

The American desert

Key
1 California Aqueduct
2 Los Angeles Aqueduct
3 Hoover Dam
4 All American Canal
5 Parker Dam
6 Imperial Dam
7 Central Arizona Project

overnight, and, when the railroad was completed in 1905, the town, on the main rail route from California to the east, flourished. The state of Nevada outlawed gambling in 1910, but by then it was too late; the games continued illegally in the saloons and bars, where giving the correct password was enough to be taken behind the scenes to play for high stakes in cards and roulette. In 1931 Nevada passed a bill to legalize gambling so that the revenue could be used to provide for schools; even today, more than 43 per cent of the state general fund comes from taxes on gambling.

So Las Vegas thrived, expanded, and drew more and more people as residents and visitors. When the rest of America was in the grip of the Great Depression, Las Vegas survived; it was in the prime position for development of the railway, and only 50 km (30 miles) away the Hoover Dam was growing. The first major engineering project of its kind, this was the most ambitious dam that had ever been built, and its 5,000 employees were close enough to Las Vegas to add to its prosperity.

Las Vegas, the ultimate playground – an artificial volcano adds to the light display

Las Vegas never looked back. The combination of gambling and wealth brought entertainment stars to perform in the hotels, casinos and theatres. Bigger and better hotel and entertainment complexes jostled for prime attraction. A replica of the Great Pyramid, an Arthurian castle and an artificial volcano have recently added to the fairyland atmosphere.

But all these people, a million residents and 20 million visitors, need water. And apart from the springs that formed the oasis, the surrounding land is a desert. So where does the water come from?

These lands receive less than 175 mm (7 in) of rain a year. The 'American Desert' refers to several regions: the Great Basin Desert that covers most of Nevada, western Utah and some of the surrounding sites; the Great Sandy Desert of southern Oregon; the Black Rock Desert of northwest Nevada and the Great Salt Lake Desert of western Utah. To the south, the Painted Desert of Arizona and the Red Desert of southern Wyoming are part of this desert system, all of which are cool deserts. Further south again, the Mohave Desert of California, the Sonora Desert of Arizona and Baja California, and the infamous Death Valley are hot deserts. This impressive list shows that a good proportion of the American West is naturally desert, dry, often parched, harsh and unforgiving.

So why do so many people live here? The cities of Las Vegas, Los Angeles, Phoenix and Tucson support populations in their millions. But, to do so, they must take water from somewhere.

People had lived in these deserts for centuries. Arizona is an arid state, yet prehistoric societies formed in the last 2,000 years that became organized communities. The Anazazi and Hohokum people lived in stone villages, *pueblos*, digging irrigation canals to manage the little water the desert could spare, growing corn, beans and vegetables. They were experts in *run-off* farming, where small dams and channels carry every last drop of rain that falls, even in a sudden storm, to their crops. The descendants of the Anazazi, the Hopi, still farm in this traditional way. But their villages were communities of hundreds instead of millions, and even so, they disappeared in the fifteenth century, leaving their pueblos to be reclaimed by the desert.

California has more variation in geography and climate, yet most of eastern California is desert. The rainfall ranges from as much as 4,400 mm (170 in) a year in the northwest of the state to virtually nothing in the desert of the southeast, with the coastal areas getting average amounts of 20–40 mm (¾–1½ in). So California does have water, but

Creating Deserts

Deserts are not fixed and constant, they come and go over time. Sometimes they are created naturally when the climate changes, but they can also be created by human activity. The balance of the ecology of a desert is so delicate that it can be disrupted before it becomes obvious what is happening.

In the 1930s, part of the Great Plains of North America were turned into a desert, in the disaster known as the Dust Bowl. This affected parts of Kansas, Oklahoma, Texas, New Mexico and Colorado. For centuries before then, the area was a natural grassland, and grass held the soil in place, stopping it being blown around by the wind. When torrential rain came, as it does in these parts, the grass stopped the soil being washed away, and its roots retained water, so even though there were long droughts the soil did not dry out.

But when farmers moved onto the land, living off homesteads, they grazed cattle on the natural grassland and began to plough their fields to grow wheat. Once the natural grasses were reduced, either by grazing or ploughing, the soil had nothing to hold it in place. By the end of the 1920s, the land had already been over-cultivated, and at the start of the 1930s there was a series of droughts that lasted for several years in total. With

The land is stripped of moisture – the Dust Bowl, Texas, 1938

nothing to hold the topsoil in place, as the crops died the wind began to strip the soil off the land.

Dust storms plagued the area, with the wind carrying so much clay and silt that it turned the sky black, the dust sometimes reaching 5,000 m (16,000 ft) into the atmosphere. In places, up 10 cm (4 in) of topsoil was blown away, and created 'black blizzards'; the wind piled up the heavier particles like sand in a similar way to a snowdrift. Some of these dust storms were huge; they even reached as far as the east coast. In 1933, a dust storm carried its dust as far as 3,200 km (2,000 miles), from Montana to the Atlantic, where black rain fell on New York State, and brown snow fell on Vermont.

The farmland became useless, and thousands of families had no choice but to abandon their homesteads. The area had become a desert, as nothing could grow there; any rain that did fall now just washed the topsoil away. The crisis occurred at the same time as the Great Depression, adding to the economic disaster.

The Dust Bowl lasted for approximately ten years, but by the middle of the 1930s efforts were made to contain the problem. Large areas were reseeded with grass, and windbreaks of trees were planted in an attempt to stop the soil erosion. Crop rotation was introduced, with a three-year cycle of wheat, sorghum, and leaving the land fallow, and by the 1940s some of the area had recovered.

not necessarily in the right place for its massive cities. Although Europeans discovered California for themselves in 1542, it was not developed right away. The area – and its Indian population – was left more or less alone for another three centuries.

Early in 1848 James Wilson Marshall, a carpenter from New Jersey, picked up nuggets of gold from the American River. California would never be the same again.

The dramatic increase in population in the second half of the nineteenth century created a demand for water. The gold rush peaked in 1852, but the settlers kept coming. In the warm climate, they could grow fruit, and the completion of the railroads – the Southern Pacific in 1876 and the Santa Fe in 1885 – meant they could ship oranges back east. Los Angeles was a fast-growing city, but it lacked two basic features: it did not have a natural harbour like San

Francisco, and it did not have enough water. Most of the rain that falls on the state falls in the north, yet the population was growing at its fastest in the south.

The harbour problem was solved by Los Angeles City acquiring a port some 37 km (23 miles) south of City Hall, including the harbour communities of San Pedro and Wilmington. The water problem was not so easily solved.

In 1904, the superintendent of the water bureau, William Mullholland, realized that an aqueduct could bring water to the city from Owens Valley, some 400 km (250 miles) northeast of Los Angeles. It would bring melted snow from the Sierra Nevada mountains to satisfy the demands of the citrus farms as well as the city itself. Despite resistance from the Owens Valley ranchers, the Los Angeles aqueduct was completed in 1913. Two syndicates of speculators were involved, and rumours of dubious wheeling and dealing plagued the project. If nothing else, it made a cracking good story which, somewhat fictionalized, was made into the movie *Chinatown*.

Although the Los Angeles Aqueduct supplies 80 per cent of the city's water, the growing city's demand for water was to grow with it. The population doubled in the 1920s. So Los Angeles also needed to take water from the California Aqueduct, 1,100 km (700 miles) of water-conveyancing system that brings fresh water from the mountains in the north of the state to the populations in the south, an arrangement not entirely approved of by the residents of the north. This aqueduct system is the main feature of the California State Water Project, which was begun in 1960, to bring water from the Sacramento River delta, east of San Francisco, to the south. It is a concrete lined canal, typically 12 m (40 ft) wide at the base and with a 9 m (30 ft) average depth of flow.

The city's thirst for water was still not satisfied, so, other than a few local wells, the rest of the water was brought from the Colorado River. But Los Angeles is not the only community taking water from the Colorado. Things are not that simple.

Which brings us back to where we came in. Where does Las Vegas get its water? As the city grew, the groundwater that created the original meadows, and provided water to the settlements that were being built there, was not enough. It would dry up unless another source of water was found. So, in 1947, the Las Vegas Valley Water District was created to build a system that would bring water from the Colorado River to the city, a system that was started in 1968. The first stage was completed in 1971, the second in 1982. And another community became dependent on the Colorado River.

The Colorado River runs for over 2,250 km (1,400 miles) across seven states before entering Mexico, and then the ocean. And one in ten Americans – including three in four people living in Arizona – receive some or all of their water from this river. It provides enough water to irrigate 15 per cent of America's crops. The Colorado River is a lifeline for most of the American West; in total, more than 25 million people in America and Mexico depend on it in some way. The first development of the river was started in 1928 with the massive, ambitious Hoover Dam, which was completed in 1936, creating the artificial lake, Lake Mead. The dam not only controls the reservoir, and the river's flood-water, it

Controlling the Colorado River – the Hoover Dam and Lake Mead

WATERING THE DESERT

also generates electricity, serving Arizona, Nevada and southern California. Since then, the river has been dammed and diverted, its water not only distributed through the states it flows through, but much of California as well. More than 20 dams now strangle the Colorado and its tributaries and its water is the cause of continual squabbling and arguing among the states and communities that lay claim to it.

The Colorado and its tributaries are called the 'Colorado River Basin', and, as there were so many conflicting claims to the water from these rivers, in 1922 the states of Arizona, California, Nevada, Colorado, New Mexico, Utah and Wyoming were party to the Colorado River Compact, an agreement that apportioned the water between the 'Upper Basin' and the 'Lower Basin'. The Upper Basin consisted of the parts of the states of Arizona, Colorado, New Mexico, Utah and Wyoming that had water draining into the river, or would take their water out of the river upstream of a point, Lee's Ferry, on the main stem of the Colorado. The Lower Basin then consisted of the rest of the states whose waters drain into, or took their water from, the system downstream of Lee's Ferry.

This made for a complicated allocation of water rights, which sustained an ongoing battle for access to the water.

In 1963, Arizona finally won confirmation of their right to take water from the Colorado. Arizona is an arid state, with high temperatures and less than 250 mm (10 in) of rain a year. In the summer, dramatic storms unleash torrential rain and flash floods, but this does not add much to the water available for use.

The city of Phoenix, in Arizona, was named because it rose out of the ashes of an abandoned Hohokum town. The original inhabitants had built a system of irrigation canals that took water from the Salt River, but they, too, had disappeared by the end of the fifteenth century. In the late nineteenth century, settlers came to south Arizona, and once more took water from the Salt River to irrigate their crops. But the Salt River was not a particularly reliable source of water, as sometimes it would flood, at other times dry up. The river was brought under control by the Roosevelt dam in 1911, when government policy was to encourage more people to settle in the American West.

After World War II, turbine pumps were introduced to the area to bring water up from *aquifers* deep underground. Aquifers are created when water seeps down through cracks and pores in rocks, collecting in the spaces between the rocks underground. This water is called groundwater, and where a spring or well gives access to this water from the surface the underground water is called an aquifer. With access to this source of groundwater, the population of Arizona grew dramatically, from just over half a million in 1945 to over 3.6 million in 1990.

Phoenix is a fast-growing city, with a dry, sunny climate; it attracts the wealthy who come to retire, and the suburbs such as Scottsdale consist of housing estates with huge lawns and swimming pools, golf courses and leisure lakes. To maintain this level of luxury, and to keep all the grass fresh and green, the sprinklers are kept on almost permanently. At one point, the residents of Scottsdale were using around 4,000 litres (900 gallons) a day – each. This was 20 times the average amount of water used in Europe. In Fountain Hills, a 150-m (500-ft) fountain sprays water into air that is so hot and dry that much of the water evaporates before it hits the ground.

Growing alfalfa in Owens Valley, California by means of a mobile irrigation system

But water in aquifers may have taken centuries to accumulate. It needs to be refreshed if the aquifer is not to dry up. Taking water from an aquifer is like mining; once it has been used up, there is nothing left. It is a non-renewable resource. And the more water that is taken the lower the water level becomes, and the lower the water level becomes the more salty the water is, making it more expensive to pump and treat. The Salt River has not provided enough water for the prosperous city for some time now, and, in an attempt to stop the aquifer being drained, a new water supply system was proposed – the Central Arizona Project.

The Central Arizona Project is a 540-km (336-mile) system of aqueducts, pipes, tunnels and siphons that zigzags through the Arizona desert, bringing water from the Colorado River as far as the San Xavier Indian Reservation southwest of Tucson. It was started in 1973, and the first water was delivered in 1985; it was completed in 1993. The water is used to supply the cities of Phoenix and Tucson,

The Vanished Ones

The deserts of southern Arizona, around the Phoenix area, were once inhabited by a people whose culture lasted for over 1,000 years. They lived off the land, their agriculture supported by a complex irrigation system. These people were the Hohokum, and their name means 'the vanished ones'; by AD 1500, the whole community had suddenly disappeared, their homes and irrigation systems abandoned.

It is thought that their settlements originated sometime between 300 BC and AD 500. They lived along the Salt River and Gila River basins, in desert that has an average summer temperature of 34°C (94°F), and only 180 mm (7 in) of rain a year. But they could support communities of hundreds of people, with a hierarchical structure to organize the digging and maintenance of their networks of canals.

The canals were wide and shallow, up to 15 km (9 miles) long, leading from the river to the mosaic of fields. They were designed with a slope of 2.5 m (8 ft) per 1.6 km (1 mile), which gives an ideal flow rate to wash out silt and stop the build-up of salts. The canals took the water from the river to the irrigation ditches that watered the fields, and an ingenious system of valves using woven mats controlled the direction of water flow. This irrigation system allowed them to grow crops of corn, beans and squash as well as cotton and tobacco. They could raise two annual crops – one in March and April, when the snow melted in the surrounding mountains, swelling the river, and the other in August when the rains came.

Montezuma's Castle – an abandoned Hohokum city

Hunting was not a major part of their lives, as they seemed to have lived on a mainly vegetarian diet, although they did occasionally supplement their food with bighorn sheep, antelope and kangaroo rats. The wild cacti of the desert provided fruits.

There was probably a strong Mexican influence on the Hohokum people, as their towns had the flat, square pyramids of the central American cultures. They also had well-established ball courts, where they played a ball game with a rubber ball, possibly acquired by trade from central America. The largest community, Snaketown, covered 120 ha (300 acres) and was occupied for as long as 1,500 years. It is thought that the Hohokum culture was as advanced as those of central America, the Maya and Aztec.

Yet the Hohokum disappeared, and no one is really sure why, although there are several theories. The large towns and villages were deserted, and the people dispersed, possibly into small groups. It could have been that the climate changed, that several droughts in succession were more than their irrigation system could accommodate. They might have suffered repeated raids from the neighbouring Apache tribes, relatively recent immigrants to the area. Whatever the reason, their descendants, the Tohona O'odum, refer to them as the 'ones who vanished', but otherwise have no explanation as to what happened. The remains of the towns and irrigation canals were found by European explorers, and the city of Phoenix grew up from the ashes of the abandoned site.

irrigate farmland and finally replenish some of the water taken from the aquifers.

Until the recent completion of the Central Arizona Project, Tucson relied entirely on groundwater for all its needs, and this water would not last for ever. Although Tucson citizens acknowledge that they *are* living in the middle of a desert, and do not demand such extensive fountains, lawns and golf courses as the citizens of Phoenix, there is still a need to be careful with water use, which is not always appreciated. When, in 1976, the city council doubled the

water bills, the uproar that followed resulted in them all being voted out of office.

Water is a basic need for all life, and to live in a region where it is naturally so scarce is to flaunt once more our control of nature. We are convinced we can live anywhere, however harsh the environment. But scarcity brings competition, rivalry, disputes and arguments; whoever controls the water controls the land, the community – controls everything. There is no way round it. As one Arizona farmer put it, 'Around here, whisky's for drinking, and water's for fighting.'

Taming the Rivers

chapter 17

Mississippi Delta, shining like a National guitar.

Paul Simon

A river is a living, changing, evolving feature of the landscape, and it has one, single purpose – to reach the sea by the fastest, easiest and simplest route. But a river does not simply carry rainwater and snow melt down to the sea, it also carries silt – finely suspended particles of mud and clay, and larger particles of soil and gravel – and herein lies a problem.

People build cities along the banks of rivers. The waterway provides a transport route, a supply of fresh water, a means of washing away waste, water for industry, even a power supply. This arrangement works well until the river either floods, or changes course, or both at the same time. And it is inevitable that the river will do one or the other.

The flow of water carried by a river is not fixed; it changes as its source changes. It may be seasonal, when snow high in the mountains begins to melt, adding to the normal water flow, or it may be carrying the result of exceptionally high rainfall somewhere along its route. When the water flow gets

'Big Muddy' – the birdsfoot delta of the Mississippi River

The Mississippi River

beyond a certain level, the river bursts its banks and spills onto the surrounding land, creating a flood-plain. The great civilization of Egypt was based entirely on the annual flooding of the Nile; not only did the floodwater bring water to irrigate the crops, but the silt carried by the river was also dumped on the land, giving a rich, fertile soil to farm.

The dumping of the river's silt onto the floodplain is a natural part of its cycle. But sometimes, if the river does not flood, the silt builds up in the riverbed itself. When this happens, the river's course to the sea becomes more shallow, so if there is another, steeper, easier way to the sea, the river will change course, leaving behind the old riverbed.

The greatest river in North America, the Mississippi, 'Old Man River' himself, behaves like any other river. Its tributaries drain the snow melt and rainwater from 31 states and two Canadian provinces. They combine, merge, to form the Ohio River to the east, and the Missouri

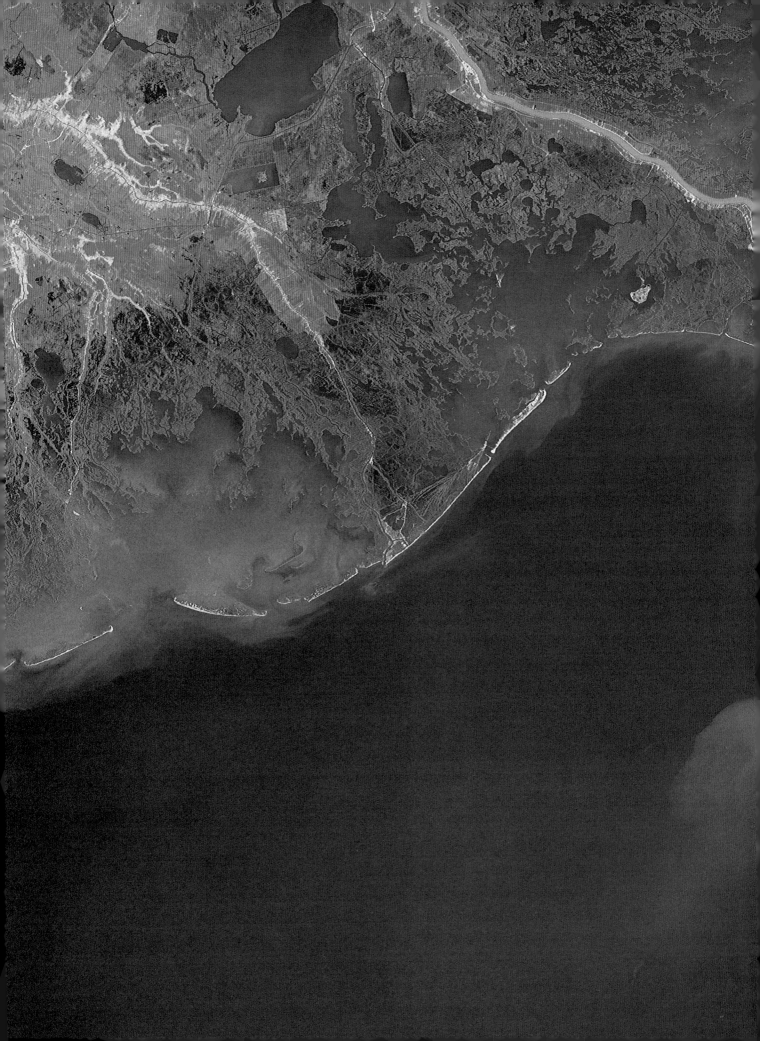

River to the west, which join the Mississippi itself at Cairo, Illinois, and St Louis, Minnesota. This mighty river, whose name derives from the Algonkian-speaking Indian's name, *Misi* ('big'), *Sipi*, ('water'), then flows south to join the Gulf of Mexico at Louisiana.

It is the major artery of the North American continent. And for thousands of years, as it flowed to the sea, the Mississippi meandered along, spilling over, changing course, searching for a way home, leaving behind parts of itself in the form of long, curved lakes, 'oxbow lakes', where a loop of the river has been cut off and abandoned, or shallow, swampy backwaters, or scars in the land where it once flowed. When it reached the Gulf coast, at Louisiana, it deposited its silt as it reached the sea, forming a patchwork of islands and wetlands. As the silt builds up on the riverbed, eventually the course becomes too shallow, so the river spills over into another channel, searching for an easier way to the sea. But it carries so much silt that the first Europeans to meet it called it 'The Big Muddy'. Most of the Mississippi's silt is fine clay particles, which form a very wet mud, and as it settles the water is squeezed out and the level sinks. But more sediment is always accumulating on top of it, so the overall level of the delta stays the same; the natural process of the river keeps the delta stable.

The lower stretch of the Mississippi has changed course every thousand years or so, creating a great triangular delta of swamps, with old river courses like threads spreading out like a fan. The waters from the river are rich in nutrients, so flocks of shore birds make their homes on the islands; pelicans, gulls and skimmers live on the fish that make the delta a haven for wildlife.

The Mississippi itself is timeless. But over the last few hundred years people have settled on its banks, and, in the blink of an eye in the river's timescale, the settlements turned into huge cities. Baton Rouge and New Orleans are cities that *seem* permanent to us. And as the cities expanded, so did the industry and commerce that supported them, until their economy came to depend on the river in some form or another.

With this sense of permanence came the need to control the river, to tame it. As early as 1699, farmers cultivating the fertile land on the floodplain found the floods themselves inconvenient, so they built a series of raised embankments, *levees* , to contain the river. In the short term, the levees worked, stopping the river flooding, sending the water on

The Mississippi flows into the Gulf of Mexico

its way downstream. The river became a main transport route, from the early paddle steamers to commercial cargo shipping, and so it had to be kept navigable. Natural vegetation was stripped from the banks, partly to let shipping through and partly to allow more cultivation of crops. But this made the banks unstable, so more engineering effort was needed to keep them maintained. All this meddling seemed to solve the problems, but in the long term things became more complicated.

Some of the river's cargo of sediment, that would normally be spread over the floodplain as the river occasionally spills over, was dropped on the riverbed instead. The level of the riverbed itself started to rise, so the river was more likely to spill over the levees and flood the farmland. Build the levees higher – the river only raises itself higher again.

There have been some very destructive floods in the history of our relationship with this wilful river. In 1882, and again in 1927, the river broke out of its chains, breached the levees, and destroyed cities, towns and many thousands of hectares of farmland. Hundreds of lives were lost and hundreds of thousands of people were made homeless. The government decided it was time to act, so in 1928 passed the Flood Control Act. Not that the river would take any notice, but it did commit the Federal Government to a positive, coordinated programme of controlling the Mississippi, rather than the piecemeal approach of people living locally along its banks.

The idea was to prepare to contain a theoretical flood, the 'project flood', that would be worse than the devastating flood of 1927. So a massive engineering project was started that eventually created more than 3,200 km (2,000 miles) of levees, about half on the Mississippi itself, and the rest on the banks of its tributaries, the Arkansas and Red Rivers. Floodways were built, so that if the river's flow rose beyond a certain amount some of the water could be diverted in a controlled way through ready-prepared channels, taking the pressure further downstream. If 'project flood' did happen, everything was ready for it.

Except that, in 1993, it all went horribly wrong. The river

**Pelicans nest on the shifting islands
of the Mississssippi Delta**

was to show who was really in charge, and all hell broke loose.

It all started in the summer, when weather patterns all over the northern hemisphere went awry, and over the central USA warm, moist, unstable air flowing north from the Gulf of Mexico met unusually cool, dry air moving south from Canada.

Warm, wet air being suddenly cooled creates rain – lots of it. So all over the Mississippi River basin torrential rainfall created the wettest June and July since 1895. Rainstorms in the Dakotas, Wisconsin and Minnesota were to dump 200 mm (8 in) of rain at once. Not only was this a lot of water, but it came suddenly, and the only place it could go was into the river systems.

The river did what it always did at times like this. It flooded. By 14 July, over 100 of the rivers that feed into the Mississippi had flooded, and the Mississippi itself had spread to 11 km (7 miles) wide. Nine states were involved, 48 lives were lost and there was over 12 billion US dollars' worth of damage. Seventy-five towns were completely submerged, some of which were flooded for 160 consecutive days. Twelve commercial airports were closed, and in Hardin, Missouri, more than 700 coffins were carried away by the floodwater.

In St Louis, the citizens watched as the floodwater rose higher and higher, and by 1 August it was only 75 cm (30 in) below the top of the flood wall, built to protect the city, and one of the strongest and highest on the Mississippi. But the water level did not recede, and the strain on the structure began to tell; it developed a leak. Emergency workers using stones and sandbags were able to stop the flow, and the flood wall held.

The 1993 floods did their damage to the regions around the upper Mississippi, upstream of Cairo. But the rains that had swelled the rivers feeding the upper Mississippi had little effect on the Ohio River that joins the main flow at Cairo. When the upper Mississippi was awash, the levels of the Ohio were lower than usual, so the total water flowing into the lower Mississippi was not so threatening. The flood-control systems designed to contain the 'project flood'

Controlling the Mississippi

In 1954, the US Congress and the Army Corps of Engineers declared war on the Mississippi. The Mississippi wanted to flow to the sea via a new route that took it along the riverbed of the Atchafalaya, but the government decided it must be stopped.

At that time, a third of the Mississippi's flow had already been grabbed by the Atchafalaya and the Army Corps of Engineers' instructions were to limit the flow to that, to stop it taking any more. In 1955, construction began of the Old River Control Project, an engineering feat that would cost 67 million US dollars and take seven years to complete. The Mississippi was tamed by a system of dams and gates, and the flow was held at the level intended – a third to the Atchafalaya, two-thirds to the Mississippi. A lock was included, so that navigation was still possible between the Mississippi, the Atchafalaya and the Red River, as before.

But in 1973 a major flood of the Mississippi nearly destroyed parts of the structure. The turbulence of the floodwater damaged the foundations and part of the wall of one of the control structures, the Lower Sill structure, and emergency repairs were needed to stop the structure from collapsing completely. Once the flood receded, more permanent repairs were completed, and an

Auxiliary Structure was built, finally completed in the mid-1980s. A power plant is operated in conjunction with the Old River Control Project, generating hydroelectric power from the difference in height between the Mississippi and Atchafalaya Rivers.

Although the structures were originally intended to keep the Mississippi on its original course, they also allow the flow of the rivers to be controlled so that, if a major flood were to threaten New Orleans, the water can be diverted into the Atchafalaya, saving the city. This would create a new problem, however. If the Mississippi waters were diverted in this way, there is no guarantee that they could be directed back again to the original Mississippi route. New Orleans would be stranded without the river passing through it.

For now, it seems that the control structures are doing their job and the Corps of Engineers are winning the war. The structures are constantly monitored, the foundations checked to ensure that the water is not causing any damage. If the structures hold, the mighty Mississippi will have been tamed, reduced to an obedient, benign

waterway, and the Atchafalaya will stay as it is, a tributary of the great river. But this means that the engineers who maintain the structures can never turn their backs on the river, can never relax their vigilance in monitoring the water levels and flow rates. The mightiest river in North America may yet find a way to satisfy its own needs and take an easier route to the sea, and it may be that in the long run we may not be able to stop it.

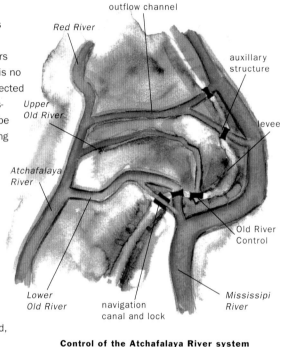

Control of the Atchafalaya River system

were able to cope with the waters pouring down the Mississippi at this stage, and the towns of Baton Rouge and New Orleans were safe.

But New Orleans depends on the Mississippi; without the river, the city would face economic disaster.

The state of Louisiana was originally a French province. In 1718, the French governor of Louisiana identified the highest ground on the delta and founded a city, a port to serve the trade from further up the river. But even the highest ground was still prone to flooding, so the answer was to build huge earthworks, up to 4.2 m (14 ft) high, around the city to keep out the river water. It worked to some degree but did not help another problem – rain. The torrential rainfall that regularly drenches the city has to go somewhere, but where? With the city below river level, there was

nowhere for the water to drain, so even when the river was behaving itself the city was awash with rainwater.

Even as late as 1899, there was no sewerage system, so until then citizens just dumped refuse directly into the river. Diseases such as typhoid and cholera were common, and mosquitoes breeding in the stagnant water spread yellow fever. It took the vision of one man to transform the city – a young engineer, A. Baldwin Wood. In his spare time, at the age of 27, he designed a pump that was the largest of its kind, with a system to stop the water backing up when the pump was not being used. The council eventually agreed to support his ideas, and by 1915 the city had 11 of the pumps installed and working. Wood went on to patent several other pump designs and his engineering feat made New Orleans famous; his original pumps are still working. The

New Orleans depends on the Mississippi for its industry and commerce

pumping system not only has to remove the water out of the city streets, but must also lift it over the surrounding levees and into the lake, to keep New Orleans dry. Between them, the city's pumps could suck the Thames in London dry.

The levees keep the waters of the Mississippi out, and are designed to withstand the theoretical 'project flood' that is thought to be the worst case scenario; life is a continual war against water. Yet, so far, New Orleans seems to be winning, as it has become more and more dependent on the Mississippi for its industry and commerce. The river is one of the busiest commercial waterways in the world, carrying cargoes such as petroleum and petroleum products, coal and coke, iron and steel, and a range of industries has grown up along its banks.

The Mississippi itself, however, has other ideas. It took over its present course about a thousand years ago, and over the centuries has built the distinctive shape called the 'bird's foot delta'. Its sediment has created wetlands and islands, in a natural process that depends on the natural flow of the river. As people have meddled with it, straightening it, taming it, they have changed the nature of the flow. Now the river water flows much faster, and instead of gently dropping its sediment at the delta, replenishing the natural settlement and sinking of the clay, it shoots out to sea and is lost in the deep waters of the Gulf of Mexico.

Louisiana is losing its coastal wetlands at an alarming rate; they are no longer being replaced by the Mississippi's sediment. Roughly 100 km^2 (40 sq. miles) disappear every year, and the situation is not helped by the practice of digging canals through the wetlands to create navigable routes.

And now, after all this time, the Mississippi wants to change its route. A distance of 160 km (100 miles) or so to the north of New Orleans, a tributary of the Mississippi, the Atchafalaya, is making a takeover bid for its waters. At the junction of the Red River, the Atchafalaya and the Mississippi, a short waterway – the Old River – allows the Mississippi's water to flow into the Atchafalaya and down to the sea by a faster, easier route, less than half the distance of the route it currently uses. If the Mississippi was allowed to have its way, all its flow would take the new route, and everywhere downstream of the junction would be left high and dry. Without the Mississippi, New Orleans would be isolated; its commerce and industry could not function.

The irony is that the Old River, the link between the Mississippi and the Atchafalaya, was created by humans in 1831. A disgruntled riverboat captain organized to have a channel dug to get around a difficult meander in the Mississippi, where it was joined by the Red River. The Mississippi flowed through the new channel, making navigation easier, but the old meander still operated, taking water from the river to the junction with the Red River and the Atchafalaya. When a 50-km (30-mile) long jam in the Atchafalaya was cleared in 1839, the flow through the Old River increased, and a century later a third of the Mississippi was flowing through this route.

The answer, then, was to stop the Mississippi from doing what it wants to. In 1950, the Army Corps of Engineers was directed to stop any more of the Mississippi flowing down this route; 13 years and 15 million US dollars later, the control structure was finished. In 1973, the Mississippi flooded and threatened the structure, so another auxiliary structure was completed in the mid 1980s at a cost of 295 million US dollars.

The city of New Orleans cannot live without the river, yet the river may ultimately be its downfall. It may flood, bringing chaos and destruction to the city, or it may abandon the city altogether, winning its battle to flow to the sea down the Atchafalaya riverbed. The fate of New Orleans is inseparable from the whims of the Mississippi, and the attempts of humans to control it.

The Red River of the North

In April 1997, another river flooded, with devastating consequences. The Red River of the North flows across North Dakota on its way to Canada, where it flows into Lake Winnipeg. It is a shallow, muddy river, named *Miswagunmewesebee* by the Chippewa Indians, meaning 'red-coloured'; it turns a dark red colour as the light catches its waters at sunrise and sunset.

The river here, in North Dakota, flows over an ancient, flat, glacial lakebed, which made the land around it very rich and fertile. The town of Grand Forks grew up where the Great Northern Railroad crossed the river, and is an important commercial centre. But the flat, fertile land that gives the surrounding land its prosperity creates the problem when the river floods. Rather like spilling a glass of wine on a polished tabletop, the floodwaters run everywhere.

The Red River of the North floods every year, as do most rivers. Normally, the local farmland is flooded and the flood drains quickly. But in the spring of 1997 the floodwaters just kept on coming, and the town of Grand Forks was inundated. More than 50,000 people left the town, as the waters invaded their homes and businesses. The aircraft hangars at the nearby Grand Forks Air Force Base provided a temporary shelter for 3,000 people, until they could arrange to go to relatives or friends.

The people who did not evacuate the town were left without a safe water supply or sewage systems; water had to be rerouted from elsewhere to supply the town. To avoid

Grand Forks, April 1997, and the Red River of the North breaks its banks

the possibility of looting, the National Guard checked the identity of anyone going into the evacuation area. But when the floodwater had settled the silence that engulfed the town brought a surreal atmosphere.

The last time that the river flooded this dramatically was in 1897. Since then, the whole approach to flood control has advanced, with the technology to control floods on the Mississippi a major contribution. But to a certain extent there is nothing that can be done when a flood of this magnitude comes.

The floodwater can take weeks to drain, and when it does recede it leaves a coating of mud over everything, and the enormous task of cleaning up. It could be another 100 years or more before the river floods like this again, but although some flooding is inevitable there is no way to predict a major flood.

So many factors affect the level of the river, from this year's spring rainfall to last year's snow, and whether it melts, and how quickly; all that can be said is that the river will go its own way in its own time.

chapter 18 Living Dangerously

Civilization exists by geological consent,

subject to change without notice.

Will Durant

The basic problem with the way we decide where to build our homes is our perception of time. We measure time over years, decades, generations, even centuries, and things that do not change in that time seem to us to be constant. When the landscape around us is the same every time we look at it, we assume it will continue to be so in the future, and when nothing has altered for hundreds of years we have a sense of permanence. But, to the Earth, a few hundred years is a blink of an eye. And if we set up home, plant our crops and build our cities on the fertile slopes of a hill, or near a mountain, we do not allow for the capricious nature of the Earth and the unseen activity below the surface.

The island of Montserrat, in the Leeward Islands of the Caribbean, has been a holiday resort, a paradise island, for decades. It is roughly 10,000 ha (40 sq. miles) of forested mountains that preside over unspoilt beaches. The climate is a pleasant 21–23°C (70–73°F), and, as it lies in the path of the northeast Trade Winds, the breeze stops the temperature from getting uncomfortably hot. The island was first sighted by Columbus in 1493, but it was not settled until the seventeenth century, by Irish Roman Catholics. In the twentieth century, celebrities came here for holidays, and rock

A pyroclastic flow from the Soufriere Hills volcano tears across the Caribbean island of Montserrat

stars came to record their albums at Air Studios, a recording facility built by George Martin, manager of the Beatles.

But for the first time in hundreds of years, in April 1996 the mountains of the Soufriere Hills suddenly erupted in a violent explosion. There was some warning; there had been some swarms of earthquakes during the few years from 1992 that suggested that the volcano was muttering to itself, and people in the southern part of the island were evacuated to the north, and safety. But it was not until April 1996 that the volcano really lost its temper. Ash was flung up to 12,000 m (40,000 ft) in the air, and a *pyroclastic flow*, a burning, searing cloud of ash, dust and shards of rock, tore down the mountain. In May, a pyroclastic flow reached the sea, where its heat boiled the water underneath and the whole cloud moved forward on a cushion of steam.

No one was hurt at this stage because of the earlier evacuation. But as with most volcanoes, even as far back as Pompeii, the volcanic ash produces a rich, fertile soil and to farm the slopes can be very productive. In Montserrat, farmers were reluctant to leave their crops that were thriving on the slopes of the mountain. The volcano continued to grumble, occasionally belching out ash clouds and intermittent pyroclastic flows.

Then, in June 1997, the volcano exploded again, and this time 19 people were killed, people who had stayed

with their farms. It was a major eruption. A series of devastating pyroclastic flows poured down the north side of the volcano, a wall of heat seared everything in its path. The flow reached almost to the Bramble airport, and a huge cloud of ash, reaching 10 km (6 miles) up into the sky drifted over to the west of the island. The abandoned capital, Plymouth, was covered in ash, as were many other farms and villages. Trees were left standing, their leaves and branches burnt away by the heat of the pyroclastic flow. The people still living on the island were forced to move further into the north, away from the volcano, away from their villages and their capital in the south. They created a new, makeshift capital in the little town of Salem, on the northwest of the island, but even this area was declared a danger zone as the volcano threatened to explode again.

It is possible that, in the long run, Montserrat will be no longer viable. By late summer 1997, the population had already declined from 11,000 to 4,000; there is serious doubt whether the taxes collected from these few could sustain the economy. As a British island colony, the people of Montserrat have looked to the United Kingdom for help, but an evacuation plan was never finalized to everyone's satisfaction. Many of the island's people felt they had nowhere to go, and although the British government offered them temporary accommodation in Britain, they would have to pay their own fares. When the volcano became more active in August, a British destroyer, *HMS Liverpool*, was standing by to evacuate the islanders to neighbouring islands, but, at the time of writing, the situation was still unresolved, and no one knows whether the people of Montserrat will, in the long run, have to concede defeat.

The Soufriere Hills volcano had not erupted in hundreds of years. Yet the islands of the Caribbean were created by volcanoes. The relentless process of plate tectonics means that the North American plate and the South American plate are crashing into the Caribbean plate, moving at about 2 cm (¾ in) a year. The island chain of the Lesser Antilles was formed when the South American plate was forced under the Caribbean plate, in the process known as *subduction*. As happens when two plates collide like this, the pressure on the descending plate melts some of the rock, which forces its way to the surface to create volcanoes. The whole arc of the Caribbean islands was formed in this way, and they are still active.

The natural harbour of San Francisco Bay was created by the parallel movement of two great tectonic plates

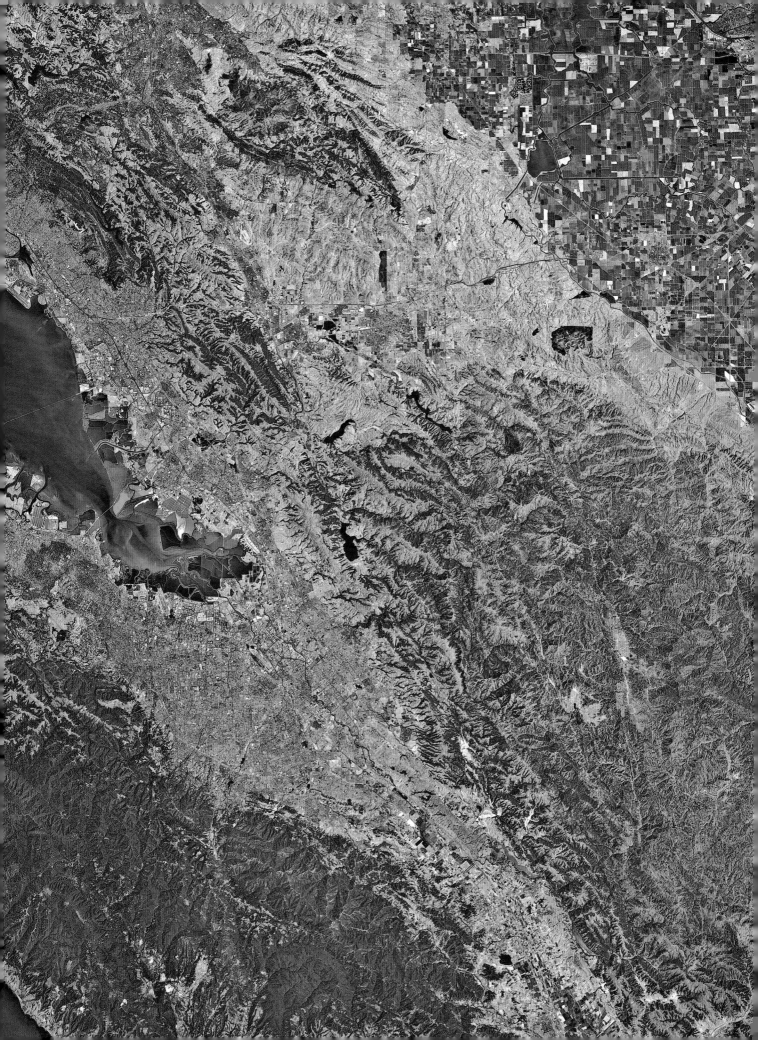

In 1902, the island of Martinique was in a similar situation to Montserrat. It had a smouldering volcano, Mount Pelee, and in the April of that year it began to shoot jets of steam and ash into the air. Some people left, but many stayed, insisting there was nothing to worry about. On 5 May, the volcano sent a scalding wave of mud into a sugar-cane factory, 1.5 km (1 mile) south of the capital, St Pierre. There was some panic, and troops guarded the roads, but on 8 May, Mount Pelee exploded without warning. It took three minutes, and the town of St Pierre no longer existed. The death toll was 28,000; two people survived. And only the day before, on the island of St Vincent, a volcano in the same chain had exploded, killing over a thousand people.

The movement of continental plates tends to take place in a timescale that is imperceptible to us. But when they slide past each other they distort the landscape, creating a 'fault'. Probably the most famous fault is created by the southeast movement of the North American plate, as it passes the Pacific plate moving northwest – the San Andreas fault in California.

The aftermath of the 'World Series' earthquake of 17 October 1989 in San Francisco

The distortion and shearing effect in what would become California produced a great natural harbour, with a sheltered bay. San Francisco.

When gold was discovered in the California hills, in 1848, the gold rush turned San Francisco from a quiet settlement into a thriving city, a busy port with a fast-growing population. Building went on as fast as the population was increasing, so by 1900 there were more than 340,000 people in the Bay Area. But in all this frenzied building under the new prosperity no one could possibly know about moving plates. There had been an earthquake in 1868, and again in 1872, but these did not prepare the city for what was to come. On 18 April 1906, the plates slipped again and a massive earthquake shook the city, destroying most of the downtown area, much of the residential area, and causing a fire that raged for three days.

It happened at 5.14 am, when most people were asleep. A few hardy souls wandering the city at night noticed that the horses seemed distressed, and dogs were barking and excited. But no one had any idea what was to happen.

Suddenly, the pavements were buckling, the buildings were collapsing, and in a brief, terrifying 60 seconds hell broke loose. When it stopped, the city was unrecognizable. Horses, driven crazy by fear, were running wild among the rubble, the dead and dying were trapped among the toppled buildings. Then, even worse than the earthquake – fire. Broken gas lines and severed electrical cables set the city ablaze. The fire department was fighting a losing battle, as the water pipes were fractured and the fire hydrants were useless. They tried to create fire breaks by blowing up some of the damaged buildings, but this only made things worse.

The fire raged for three days, destroying of the business district and more than half of the residential areas. Part of the problem that made the city so vulnerable was that much of the housing had been built on landfill sites; areas of swampland that had been filled in with debris, soil, wood and rubbish from the days of the gold rush. These areas could not withstand the shaking, and much of the building collapsed. Original reports suggested that 700 people died, but the final death toll may have been as high as 2,000; no one will ever really know for sure. The combination of the quake and the fire live on in history as the 'Big One', and if it can happen once it can happen again.

The city was rebuilt, and life went on as before. Yet, before long, the same problem that had caused so much damage in 1906 was to have disastrous consequences. On 17 October 1989, the World Series baseball game between the San Francisco Giants and the Oakland Athletics was to be played at the Candlestick Park in San Francisco. A crowd of 60,000 was in the stadium and the game was being televised live for millions of viewers. Both teams had completed their batting practice and there were 20 minutes to go before the start of the big game. But, at 5.04 pm, the same part of the fault that had caused the 'Big One' slipped again. An earthquake shook the stadium, watched by millions of viewers as it happened.

This was a 7.1 magnitude earthquake, which lasted only 11 seconds, but it still did some serious damage. The magnitude of an earthquake is measured on a logarithmic scale, which simply means that an increase of 1 on the scale refers

Predicting Earthquakes

The problem with predicting earthquakes is that they are unpredictable; being unpredictable, no one can be there, waiting to study them as they happen. Bill Bocken is a geophysicist who is very aware of this problem.

Earthquakes are a very interesting phenomenon. We can't predict them, and they happen infrequently. When we want to learn something about an earthquake, we can put all the instruments out that we can think of, and then we essentially have to wait for the earth to do its thing.

Parkfield, a small town, sits directly on top of the St Andreas fault in California.

Parkfield has been monitored for a number of years. It was always a very interesting site. But in the 1980s new information was developed on older Parkfield earthquakes that suggested that Parkfield was a special site. It was special in that earthquakes tended to occur on a very regular time frame, about every 22 years. The other interesting thing is that all the information suggested that Parkfield earthquakes were very similar. What happened in an earlier earthquake tended to happen in the next one. So it provided a unique oppor-

tunity to focus on the most likely place in California for the next damaging earthquake, and also to know something about the important characteristics of that earthquake before it happened. And that allowed us to design experiments that would focus on these very special places and possibilities.

So Parkfield became the home of the Earthquake Prediction Experiment. Cameras and measuring instruments were placed so that they would be triggered by the slightest vibration, and so if the earthquake happened again they would record the whole event.

In the early days of the experiment, we were rushing to get the instruments in place because we weren't sure when the earthquake would happen and the most likely time was about 1988.

The only snag with this was that the earthquake did not happen. It did not occur in 1988 and has not happened in the subsequent ten years. Parkfield is still waiting. California has suffered serious earthquakes elsewhere – one in 1989 and another in 1994 – but Parkfield's major event has yet to arrive. The geophysicists and seismologists all work on monitoring other projects as well, but for detailed measurements they

Parkfield town occupies a special site – right over the San Andreas Fault, California

wait for the Earth to move at Parkfield. There is no point in moving the instrumentation to another site. Bill Brocken again:

The instrumentation that one would want to install in such an experiment is already here, it can't be moved elsewhere. Many of the expensive pieces of equipment are cemented in place 200 metres below the Earth's surface; they can't be moved.

Sometimes we can wait an awfully long time. At Parkfield we thought we would have to wait a few years and it turned out that we've waited somewhat longer than that. I certainly am tired of waiting for this earthquake, and it's time for it to happen.

to an increase in earthquake strength of ten-fold. The quake of 1906 was estimated at 8.25, which makes it well over ten times more destructive than this one of 1989. But even so, 67 people were killed, over 3000 injured and 12,000 people made homeless. And on the northern shore of the city the elegant Marina residential district was a reminder of the 1906 disaster. Much of the area was again built on landfill, some even left over from 1906, and this artificial fill amplifies the shock waves from the quake. The shock waves also turned the material momentarily to liquid. When the quake was over, and the damage assessed, it was found that many of the buildings that had survived the quake had to be demolished, as their foundations were unstable.

The other main disaster was the collapse of 1.6-km (1-mile) long double section of an elevated roadway, the Interstate 880. Forty-two people died in their cars as 44

concrete slabs dropped onto the lower road, crushing anything below. The section had been built on relatively soft mud, which amplified the shock waves, and flaws in the design on the roadway meant that the supports were not reinforced properly. The tragedy is a result of the eternal conflict between building for safety, in this case to withstand the inevitable earthquakes, and saving cost.

Americans on the west coast have lived with earthquakes for a few centuries; across the Pacific, in Japan, people have endured earthquakes for thousands of years. Like California, Japan is on the 'Ring of Fire', the circumference of the Pacific, where the Earth is at her most active, where the boundaries of moving plates create earthquakes and volcanoes. Mount Fuji, Japan's sacred mountain, is a dormant volcano that last erupted in 1708.

And, like California, Japan is subject to earthquakes.

Much time and money is poured into the technology of earthquake prediction. In 1995, the Fourth Japan-US Workshop on Urban Earthquake Hazard Mitigation was held in Osaka and was due to start on 17 January. But at 5.46 am the Osaka Bay area was hit by a massive, unpredicted earthquake. It was a magnitude 7.1, the same as the World Series 'quake in San Francisco, but this earthquake was focused near the city of Kobe, and the damage was horrific. The immediate death toll was over 5,000.

Kobe is a busy, industrial port, built along a strip of coast on Osaka Bay. Once more, some of Kobe was built on landfill, and once more the shock waves caused it to liquefy. And, like the 1906 quake of San Francisco, much of the damage was due to fire. Broken fuel pipes, electric heaters – even aquarium heaters – all contributed to the fire; the fire services were hampered by fractured water mains and difficult access to reach the fires. The buildings that collapsed were usually the older ones, built before new

regulations made them more resistant to earthquakes.

Also in Japan, and also prone to earthquakes, is Tokyo. Although badly damaged in 1923, Tokyo is waiting for a 'Big One'. With new building practice and awareness, if it happened now, the loss of life would be lower than may have been estimated until recently. But there is another problem, one that could affect the whole world. If a serious earthquake were to rock Tokyo, in a worst-case situation, the cost of repairing the damage could run into trillions of dollars. To rebuild Tokyo, the Japanese would have to withdraw the money they have invested in international projects and businesses. If they were to do that, there would be a major financial crash that would send the international markets into chaos and rock the world economy.

Dormant Mount Fuji is a relic of Japan's geological activity, the full power of which was felt in Kobe in 1995

chapter 19

The Long Winter

Some say the world will end in fire, some say in ice

From what I've tasted of desire

I hold with those who favour fire.

But if it had to perish twice, I think I know enough of hate

To say that for destruction, ice

Is also great. And would suffice.

'Fire and Ice' — *Robert Frost*

Right now, at the end of the twentieth century, we are in the middle of an ice age. True, the icesheets only cover the poles, and true, we seem to be enjoying a relatively mild climate, but ice ages come and go with a rhythm of their own, in a timescale outside our experience.

What *is* an 'ice age'? The answer is not as simple as it seems. Several times in the history of the Earth, the temperature has been low enough for huge icesheets to cover much of the surface of the planet. An ice age lasts for a few million years, and there seems to be one roughly every 150 million years. These are huge periods of time – it is hard to comprehend the idea of a few million years here or there. When the dinosaurs walked the Earth, 250 million years

An ice age – millions of years of bitter cold

ago, most of the land was covered in tropical vegetation; the planet was between ice ages then, and enjoyed tropical and subtropical climates.

Yet there have been several of these ice ages. Around 435 million years ago, icesheets covered much of Brazil, North Africa and across to Yemen and Saudi Arabia. And 600 million years ago another ice age held the planet in its grip. The most recent ice age started about 2.5 million years ago, at the start of what is called the *Quaternary* period.

Ice ages are complicated because the period is not just one of long, intense, bitter cold. Within an ice age, there are cycles of changing temperatures that repeat over and over. In a cycle of about 100,000 years, there are short periods of relative warmth, when the icesheets retreat towards the poles, and the temperature rises slightly; this period is called an *interglacial* and lasts 10,000 years or so. Then the Earth cools again, and the ice reclaims the planet, until 100,000 years later, when the pattern repeats itself again.

The ice age that began a few million years ago has seen ten or so repeats of this pattern in the last million years, and the pattern was not very different in the million years or so before that. And today we are reaching the end of a 10,000-year interglacial.

Many scientists believe that the repeating pattern is not yet over.

To relate this to human history, everything that we know as 'civilization', from agriculture to *Apollo 11*, has happened within the last 10,000 years, that is within this interglacial. Humans certainly lived and prospered before then, but they lived in small, mobile communities survived mainly by hunting, and by gathering wild plants. They could use tools, and they could make clothing from animal skins that protected them against the cold, but the first cities did not appear until 8,000 years ago. The gradual transition between hunter-gatherer societies and more settled, complex agricultural societies was one which developed over several thousand years. It was not until 3000 BC, that Sumerian society was stable enough to be the first to become literate.

So our experience of civilization does not really take into account the effect of a full glacial period. We are dependent on our technology, on highly specialized skills, and we are progressively cutting ourselves off from the natural world. What would happen if the ice age came back? What changes would we have to make? Could we adapt?

During an ice age, the whole planet is affected. Water is locked in the huge icecaps, which means the sea level is significantly lower. Even today, in the interglacial, three-quarters of the Earth's fresh water is locked up in icesheets and glaciers; if all this ice were to melt, the sea level round the world would rise by 90 m (300 ft). So during a glacial period, when ice extends over much more of the globe, the

Extent of ice cap during the last glacial period

sea level would be lower than it is today, and the sea would be much saltier.

Glaciers form wherever more snow falls than can melt away. And glaciers are not just static lumps of ice, they move, and in doing so they reshape the landscape. They can be thousands of metres thick; the icesheet over Antarctica is more than 2 km (1¼ miles) deep, and ice is very heavy. It gives the appearance of a solid, but it is *plastic*; over time, it will flow and change shape. Some glaciers behave like rivers of ice, trying to flow downhill to reach the sea, and as they do so they gouge out valleys, grinding their way forward, leaving rich, fertile debris as they go. The movement of glaciers is so great it can shear the tops off mountains and create new valleys.

The reasons for the dramatic changes in the Earth's climate that create ice ages are only just being understood. Over a very long term, this may be due to the position of the solar system within the galaxy. The sun is a star on the outer limb of the galaxy, and, in the same way that the planets orbit the sun, the stars rotate as the galaxy spins on its axis. This whole cycle takes about 300 million years, and as the galaxy rotates our sun is carried through different densities of inter-stellar dust, through variations in gravitational and magnetic fields. In the same way that the motion of the Earth and moon create two tides, so these differences in the galaxy occur symmetrically, so changes affect the Earth twice in the cycle, every 150 million years. As the solar system passes through a more dense region of dust, the amount of sunlight reaching the Earth is slightly reduced, which can create a cooling effect.

There are many other factors involved in plunging the Earth into an ice age. As the ancient continents drifted across the globe, ocean currents were disrupted. The southern landmasses of Gondwanaland drifted north and collided with the landmasses of Laurasia. Before this happened, a warm ocean current circled the globe, distrib-

A glacier makes its way towards the sea

White snow reflects the sun's heat back into space, so the more snow there is, the more the Earth is cooled

uting heat; when Africa joined with Europe and Asia, and South America joined with North America, this current was blocked, and the new oceans, the Atlantic and Pacific, were now open to the cold currents from the poles. At the same time, Australia separated from Antarctica and the cold Antarctic current could now encircle the whole planet. Changes in ocean currents created dramatic changes in climate, possibly cooling the Earth enough to contribute to the ice age.

Once the planet does start to cool, the effect is amplified by different processes. White snow reflects the sun's heat back into space, so the more snow there is the more the

Earth is cooled. More water falls as snow, and so the Earth is cooled further. So a small, initial reduction in temperature sets off this chain reaction.

Probably more important to us on a practical level is the cause of the glacial–interglacial cycle. For more than a century, it was recognized that there was a connection between these patterns and slight variations in the Earth's orbit round the sun. But until recently there was no explanation as to *why* these changes created such major changes in the climate.

The Earth's orbit around the sun is not an exact circle; it varies between a circle and an ellipse. An *ellipse* is a shape formed when a circle is deformed. The easiest way to see one is to take, say, a wine glass (empty) and hold it up so that you can see the rim as a straight line. Now start to tilt

eccentricity of the Earth's orbit follows a cycle of 93,408 years, and this period can be seen in the patterns of glacials and interglacials.

A second variation is the tilt of the Earth as it goes round the sun; in Chapter 11 we saw how it is this 23.5° tilt that creates the seasons. But this angle is not fixed, it changes slightly, as if the Earth was nodding; it varies between 22° and 25°, and as this tilt increases the seasons will be more extreme. This cycle takes place over 41,000 years.

The third variation in the Earth's variation is the *precession of the equinoxes,* the effect seen in Chapter 11 whereby the Earth wobbles like a spinning top, so that the north pole points to different parts of the sky. It seems to trace a circle that takes 26,000 years. This will affect the temperature of the Earth because, currently, the Earth is slightly closer to the sun when it is winter in the northern hemisphere, so the winters and summers are mild. But, 11,000 years ago, it was the other way round, and the southern hemisphere had mild seasons while the north had more extremes. Because there is more land in the north, the sea does not have a chance to modify the extreme tempera-

The Earth's orbit is an ellipse which varies in shape, so the distance from the sun varies over a period of 93,408 years

The angle of the Earth's tilt is varying, so the seasons change in an extreme nature over a period of 41,000 years

The precession of the equinoxes – the Earth 'wobbles' on its axis over a period of 26,000 years

The Earth's orbit is an ellipse which varies in shape, so the distance from the sun varies over a period of 93,408 years

the glass towards you until you are looking at the rim as a circle; the shape between the line and the circle is the ellipse, and, depending on the tilt of the glass, it will appear long and thin, or round, nearly like the circle. This variation away from the circle shape is the *eccentricity* of the ellipse, and mathematicians do wonderful things with equations to describe this shape. Now, the Earth's orbit varies between being an almost perfect circle and an ellipse, and back again to a circle; when it is an ellipse it will be nearer the sun at some parts of the year than others.

This effect is *almost* so small as to be not worth mentioning, and it certainly does not create the seasons as some people mistakenly imagine. But there are factors that amplify this; snow cover is one, and there is another effect, which will be explained later. For now, this change in tures. More ice and snow forms on land in the winter, and as we have already seen, the more snow there is the colder it gets, and the Earth cools down.

These three cycles were described in detail by a Yugoslav scientist, Milutin Milkanovitch (1879–1958) who tried to explain the cycles of glacial and interglacial periods within an ice age. He did most of his work in the years before World War II, matching the patterns in the ice age with the three variations in the Earth's orbit. But although his work was known it was not taken seriously for some time because although the patterns matched neither he nor anyone could explain the *cause* of the changes. The reflecting snow effect accounted for some of it, but not all of it, and the actual changes in the orbit itself could not account for more than a degree of temperature change. So the idea stayed as nothing more than an interesting puzzle.

Then, in the 1970s, scientists began to study cores drilled out of ancient ice of glaciers and icesheets. When snow first falls, it is light and fluffy, and traps a lot of air, but as further snow falls on top, it gets packed down, and another layer forms on top. A column of ice, or core, shows successive years like the rings in a tree trunk, and can be used to count the years, and hence the age, of the ice.

Swiss researchers from the University of Bern studied the old air trapped in tiny bubbles in the layers of ice, and as they did so they found that about 20,000 years ago, when the current ice age was at its coldest, there was less carbon dioxide in the air than, say, 16,000 years ago, when the current interglacial was starting. We have met carbon dioxide before; it is one of the infamous greenhouse gases, trapping the sun's heat in the atmosphere and warming the planet.

Why did the level of carbon dioxide change? Sixteen thousand years ago, the culprit was not heavy industry, nor the traffic on the roads, so much in debate today. Back then it was a natural process in that phytoplankton, the microscopic plants that live in the surface layers of the ocean, absorb carbon dioxide to make their shells of calcium carbonate. When they die, their bodies sink to form sediment, that eventually becomes rock. It is possible that small changes in temperature can cause changes in ocean currents. If the temperature dropped slightly, that changing flow of ocean currents could provide the plankton with more nutrients, so their numbers would increase. They would take up more carbon dioxide and the Earth would cool down.

It is possible that the action of the plankton in the oceans may create changes in the planet's temperature.

Sea Ice

Seawater, being salty, does not freeze until the temperature drops below −1.9°C (28°F). But at the North and South Poles, in the bitter cold, sea ice is an important factor in driving the deep-water ocean currents that disperse heat around the planet.

When the sea is in contact with very cold air, it first begins to freeze at the surface, but only fresh water freezes. Tiny crystals of ice, only a few millimetres across, give the sea a greasy appearance, and this stage is sometimes called *grease ice*.

If the sea is fairly calm, these frozen crystals combine to give a layer of ice, up to 10 cm (4 in) thick, but if the sea is disturbed by wind and waves the ice forms pancakes up to 3 m (10 ft) across, which eventually stick together to form a continuous sheet. But this sheet of ice is very rarely smooth and even.

Wind and waves will break up large icesheets into *floes*. These sometimes separate, opening up narrow channels of water, called *leads*. If new ice forms over these leads, it will be thin and weak compared to the ice of the floes; this can be a lethal hazard to anyone trying to travel across the sea ice.

Alternatively, the leads can open up, creating a larger, more permanent area of open water, known as a *polynya*. Ships can sometimes get caught in these areas of open water, because as the ice floes keep moving they can close in on the ship, trapping it in the ice.

When the floes collide, they override each other, or the ice crumples, rather like a mountain chain being formed by plate tectonics. These collisions create huge ridges, *pressure ridges*, which are up to 10 m (33 ft) high, making the crossing of sea ice difficult as well as dangerous. But underneath a pressure ridge is a submerged 'keel' of ice, like the keel of a sailing boat, that extends downwards up to five times the height of the ridge.

The formation and melting of sea ice has implications far beyond the frozen oceans of the polar areas. The freezing of sea ice leaves behind the salt in the unfrozen water, making it more saline. This cold, saline water sinks, creating the deep-water currents that move slowly along the bottom of the oceans, the great conveyor belt of cold deep water that takes hundreds of years to complete its cycle. But these deep-water currents also move heat around the planet, affecting the climate.

If the sea ice at the poles starts to melt, fresh water is added to the seawater, making it less salty. The water now does not sink so easily and the deep-water currents can be disrupted. If global warming causes the sea ice at the poles to melt, we do not know what the long-term effect will be on the deep ocean currents, and, ultimately the Earth's climate.

Along with the changing amounts of snow cover, the plankton could amplify the tiny changes in temperature created by the changes in the Earth's orbit. The amount of carbon dioxide in the atmosphere is the crucial factor in determining whether the Earth will warm up, or whether we will be plunged back into another glacial period.

If the pattern repeats itself, as it has done for two million years, we will return to a glacial period. Icesheets will advance on North America, Asia and Europe, and polar bears will find a home in London or New York.

But – and it is a very big 'but' – the Earth does not seem to be cooling down as we would expect as we come out of this interglacial period. It seems to be warming up. And the difference between the Earth of 100,000 years ago and now is *us*. Which brings us to the much discussed question of global warming. If it will stop us returning to the long winter of an ice age, is that not a good thing?

If the pattern of glacials and interglacials repeats as before, there could be polar bears as far south as London and New York

So what is all the fuss about? The answer is that we do not know. On the one hand, some of the ideas of Gaia predict that plankton will buffer these changes of temperature; on the other hand, there is the theory that plankton could amplify these changes. As yet, there is no definite answer. We do not have any idea at all of what we are doing, and of the long-term consequences of increasing the greenhouse gases in the atmosphere. We do not know if changes in the climate are part of a natural cycle, or whether they are caused by us burning fossil fuels and generating greenhouse gases.

However, the Earth does seem to be warming up, and it does seem to be us causing it. We are like children playing with matches.

chapter 20

Playing with Matches

When you look out the other way toward the stars you realize

it's an awful long way to the next watering hole.

The Home Planet – *Loren Acton, US astronaut*

In the complicated pattern of the ocean currents, one current has become infamous in the last few decades – El Niño, the 'boy child'. El Niño is a counter-current, a disruption in the ocean currents that occur on the eastern side of the Pacific Ocean, but its effect is felt all over the world.

by the tropical sun, away from the land across to the west side of the ocean.

This warm water, with the moist Trade Winds, brings rain to Indonesia and northwestern Australia, supporting the rich rainforest. This air then rises, flowing back towards

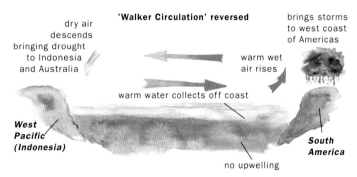

Normal conditions in the Pacific Ocean

Full El Niño conditions in Pacific Ocean

In the normal state of affairs, the swirling ocean gyre of the Pacific creates a cold current, the Humboldt, or Peru current, that flows north up the west coast of South America. The Trade Winds tend to blow towards the west, off the coast, and as they do, they push the surface water, warmed

Humans have changed the face of the planet to suit themselves more in the last millennium than in the last few million years

the east, and over Peru the descending dry air creates a desert. The circulation of air is called the 'Walker circulation', after Sir Gilbert Walker, the British meteorologist who first described this in the 1930s. Off the shores of Peru, the cold water wells up from below to replace this warm water, cold water from the deep that is very rich in nutrients, so the waters off Peru are teeming with marine life. Peru itself based its fishing industry on this effect; it has the largest fishing fleet in the world, catching anchovies that are turned into fish meal and exported as a food supplement for livestock.

It was known since the sixteenth century that, in December, a warm, south-flowing counter-current could temporarily displace this cold water. This warm current would arrive around Christmas, so it was named *la corriente de El Niño* ('the current of the boy child'). The warm water was very poor in nutrients, so the marine life suffered. El Niño was a brief annual disruption of the normal fishing conditions.

But by the end of the nineteenth century it was recognized that every three to five years this El Niño current arrived earlier, stayed for longer, and, when this happened, the productivity of the ocean fell dramatically. Eventually, the name 'El Niño' began to be applied to the exceptional years rather than the original annual event. The south-flowing warm water brought mayhem to the fishing industry, and torrential rain to the northern desert of Peru.

El Niño creates devastating drought in the Sahel Desert of Africa

What actually happens during an El Niño event? Instead of the Trade Winds blowing the surface layer of warm water to the east side of the Pacific, these winds weaken, so the warm water backs up; the surface layer of warm water becomes thicker, and eventually the winds blow in the opposite direction, from west to east, pushing the warm water back towards South America. This water can be 8–10°C (14–18°F) above normal.

Now, this creates several effects that disrupt the weather. The warm, wet air is now blowing towards Peru, creating torrential rain and storms, whereas Australia and Indonesia experience the sinking, dry air that creates drought instead of rainforest.

In 1972–1973, a particularly strong El Niño event caused such disruption that Peru's anchovy yields fell to a fraction of their normal amount; export of fish meal fell, and not only was Peru's economy seriously damaged but the world market was also affected.

The disruptions in the wind patterns of the southern Pacific were recognized by Walker and named the 'South-ern Oscillation'. At the time, he did not connect the change in pattern with El Niño's change in ocean currents, but once the connection was made this reversal in the normal patterns became known as the El Niño/Southern Oscillation, or ENSO.

El Niño rose to fame, however, in the later part of the twentieth century. A particularly extreme event happened in 1982–1983, when Australia suffered its worst drought on record, and with the drought came a vast, dust storm which choked Melbourne. Eastern Borneo was ablaze, burning a total area larger than Switzerland, and the 'Ash Wednesday' fires in South Australia and Victoria caused the loss of 76 lives and over 2,000 residential homes. At the other extreme, torrential rains fell over the central Pacific Ocean, instead of to the west where they normally fall, and there were freak storms on some of the Pacific islands. California suffered vicious winter storms, floods devastated the wheat harvest in southern China, and rainfall drenched Brazil and the southwest USA. And the Sahel Desert in Africa suffered drought, famine and death.

But then, at the beginning of the 1990s, El Niño's pattern changed. Instead of coming every few years, El Niño lasted for five years.

Southeast Australia became tinder dry. And in January 1994, in the state of New South Wales, bush fires claimed a large part of the east coast of Australia. Although fire is a natural part of the ecology of the area, these fires spread quickly and threatened the outskirts of Sydney itself. Between 27 December 1992 and 16 January 1994, 800 fires started, and they came closer to the residential areas around Sydney than ever before. The wind was blowing from the northwest, bringing more dry air that fed the fires – and no promise of rain. Every state offered and sent help, and at the height of the crisis more than 20,000 people were involved in fighting the fires.

For such a devastating event, only four lives were lost, and fewer than 200 homes destroyed. These were by no means the worst bush fires that Australia has suffered, but they captured international media attention because they

came so close to threatening a city. And they were the result of the extended El Niño/Southern Oscillation event. Which brings us to the question – *why* is El Niño doing this? The answer is that we have no idea. But a niggling doubt arises. Could it be due to global warming? For whatever reason, the Earth has been warming up in the last decade of the twentieth century, and we cannot say for sure that we – humans – have nothing to do with it. Some scientists now think that the disruption to the El Niño/Southern Oscillation pattern *could* be due to global warming brought on by our producing too much of the greenhouse gases. The possibility is there, and we cannot ignore it.

Where are the greenhouse gases coming from? The three gases that cause the most concern are carbon dioxide,

El Niño brought drought and fire to New South Wales, Australia, in 1992 and again in 1997

methane and nitrous oxide. Carbon dioxide is produced by burning coal, petroleum and natural gas – the *fossil fuels.* These were formed roughly 300 million years ago, in the Carboniferous period, when plants and animals died and decomposed, forming layer upon layer, trapped in the bottom of lakes where there was no oxygen to speak of. More sediment was laid down on top of these layers and, deep underground, this organic material was transformed into coal, oil or natural gas. We dig up this coal and oil, and tap the supplies of natural gas; by processing oil we get petroleum, and petroleum-based products. When we burn these fuels, the carbon that was part of the plants and animals that lived 300 million years ago is released back into the atmosphere, mainly as carbon dioxide.

So the use of fossil fuels by industry, and the emissions from aircraft, shipping, and the world's billions of cars, increases the total amount of carbon dioxide; and, once released, it stays in the atmosphere for 100 years. Methane is released into the atmosphere when bacteria break down organic matter in the absence of oxygen, such as in flooded rice paddy fields, landfill garbage sites and the inside of cows. Although it only stays in the atmosphere for ten years

before being broken down, methane absorbs up to 30 times the amount of heat that carbon dioxide does, making a substantial contribution to global warming.

And nitrous oxide, known better as 'laughing gas', is produced by burning fossil fuels, and by microbes in the soil; its recent increase has come from the use of chemical fertilizers in agriculture.

In December 1997, negotiators from the world's industrial nations met at Kyoto, Japan, to discuss the problem. They were trying to agree on national targets to reduce carbon dioxide emissions, using the 1990 emission figures

as a baseline and aiming to have achieved the agreed reductions by the year 2010. The proposed figures included an 8 per cent cut in emissions by the European Union, a 5 per cent cut for the USA, Japan and Russia, and a 5 per cent increase for Australia and Norway. If these figures were met, it would result in a 5 per cent cut overall in carbon dioxide emissions from the industrialized nations.

But as soon as the negotiations began, various opt-out clauses were suggested. America – in the stranglehold of the automobile industry – proposed they should be able to 'buy' carbon 'credits' from other countries that were not using their full quotas. There was also the suggestion that industrialized countries contributed to a 'clean development fund', a scheme to help developing countries set up energy systems that did not involve greenhouse gas emissions, such as wind turbines. In principle this was accepted as a good idea, but then some rich nations wanted to be able to use their contributions to the scheme to offset credits against their carbon dioxide emissions....

In the normal scheme of things, some of the carbon dioxide is reabsorbed by the planet's vegetation. This includes the huge tropical rainforests, but also includes microscopic plants that live in the surface layers of the oceans. Clearing forests – particularly tropical rainforests – not only releases more carbon dioxide into the atmosphere, as forests are often cleared by burning, but reduces the planet's capacity to reabsorb the carbon dioxide already present. At the Kyoto conference, there were suggestions that countries prepared to protect forests, or plant new ones, should also gain 'carbon credits', even though this is already an obligation under a previously agreed climate convention. And there is always the concern that this could provide the incentive to clear old, natural forests to replant new ones to clock up carbon credits.

Some issues were not even addressed at Kyoto; they had to wait for the 1998 convention in Buenos Aires. The emissions from aircraft and shipping were not addressed, and the three greenhouse gases debated in Kyoto are not the only ones causing concern. Gases called CFCs and hydro fluorocarbons also contribute to global warming, as well as damaging the layer of ozone that protects us from dangerous solar radiation. They were not considered until 1998. Despite the mounting evidence that we *are* changing the climate, we seem reluctant even to begin to change our energy-intensive lifestyles.

There are no easy answers. No one is even sure exactly what will happen if global warming does take a hold. It could be that the polar icecaps will grow bigger, as warmer conditions will cause more water to evaporate, falling as snow at the poles. Or, if the icecaps start to melt, the extra fresh water at the poles could disrupt the deep ocean currents, the Antarctic Bottom Water and the Atlantic Deep Water flows. We have seen what can happen when the pattern of a surface current like El Niño changes. No one knows what might happen if the deep ocean currents were

Clearing tropical rainforest by burning releases more carbon dioxide into the atmosphere, at the same time reducing the planet's capacity to reabsorb it

altered. And, if the Gulf Stream were disrupted, without the influence of this huge, warm current western Europe and the eastern USA could be plunged into an ice age of their own.

We tend to think that if things were to go horribly wrong, then 'nature' will be threatened, that the environment will be damaged irrevocably. Nothing could be further from the truth. Nature – life in general – is phenomenally tough; it has survived far more dramatic changes than we can impose on the planet. Life simply adapts to the new conditions and carries on. Landmasses have moved around the globe, sea levels rose and fell, huge meteors and comets hit the Earth, average temperatures varied from tropical to freezing. Extinction and evolution are opposite sides of the same coin. No, it is not nature that will suffer if we get it wrong, it is *us*.

And we are not the first to face this dilemma.

There have been many civilizations before us that have been convinced they knew what they were doing. Take the Maya, for example.

They lived in Central America, mainly on the Yucatan peninsula, and flourished from AD 300–900. They lived in cities, developed a highly sophisticated system of hieroglyphic writing, and used a precise, complex calendar to organize their year. They worshipped a pantheon of sun-, moon- and rain-gods, at huge temple sites with magnificent stone pyramids such as Chichen Itza. They were, perhaps, the most advanced of the people that inhabited Central America before the arrival of the Europeans. A sacred book, the Popol Vuh, is part of their heritage; its title means 'The Collection of Written Leaves'. It is written in the Qiche language, a dialect of the ancient Mayans.

The first three books of the *Popol Vuh* tell the story of the gods, of Creation, of how the first humans were created. By the beginning of the third book, the gods are considering their creation, the four men that were moulded from a paste of yellow and white maize. But the god Hurakan was not impressed with his creation, and complained that the men were becoming too much like the gods themselves:

> *'They understand everything perfectly, they see the four sides, the four corners in the sky, on the earth....*
> *"We have understood everything, great and small," the men said.'*
>
> *So Hurakan said: 'What shall we do with them now?' As if breathing on a mirror, he clouded their*

vision. *'Let their sight reach only to that which is nearby, let them see only a small part of the face of the Earth. Are they not just simple creatures of our own making? Must they always be gods?'*

By the end of the first millennium, the Mayan civilization had completely disappeared. Vanished. The huge stone cities were suddenly abandoned, with no obvious explanation. It is a mystery that has puzzled archaeologists and historians for centuries.

But it is now thought that the problem had been building up for some time; the population increased steadily, with rivalry between city states. It may have reached five

million in a land that now only supports thousands. The people living in the cities had to be fed, and the soil in the low-level rainforest where they lived was not fertile. As the jungle was cleared to provide fuel and fields for crops, the land became vulnerable to erosion, and as the population increased more and more land was used. The ruling classes in the cities were out of touch with what was happening, so the situation deteriorated; as crop yields fell, competition for food became more and more intense. Eventually the system collapsed, and the cities were abandoned in a matter of a few decades. A few peasant farmers stayed, but the remains of the great civilization was claimed by the jungle, only discovered again in the nineteenth century.

The ruined Mayan cities of Central America are a monument to a great civilization that went before us

The Maya failed to adjust to the gradual changes that were taking place in their environment; they were cut off from the world that sustained them. Are we set to follow them? Life, nature, Gaia – call it what you want – will survive, in some form or another, with or without us. We can live with the forces and processes of nature that shape the planet, or we can live against them, trying to impose our will on the world around us.

It is our choice.

Must we always be gods?

Bibliography

This is a list of books that have been used in the research for this book and are recommended for further reading.

Abbott, Patrick L., *Natural Disasters*. WCB, 1996.

Atkinson and Gadd, *Weather*. Weidenfeld & Nicolson, 1987.

Beckwith, Martha, *Hawaiian Mythology*. University of Hawaii Press, 1976.

Burroughs *et al.*, *Weather – the Ultimate Guide to the Elements*. HarperCollins, 1996.

Carter, Geraldine, *The Illustrated Guide to Latin American Mythology*. Studio Editions, 1995.

Carwardine, Mark, *Iceland – Nature's Meeting Place*. Iceland Review, 1996.

Cattermole and Moore, *The Story of Earth*. Cambridge University Press, 1985.

Coch, Nicholas K., *Geohazards – Natural and Human*. Prentice-Hall, 1995.

de Blij, H. J., *Nature on the Rampage*. Smithsonian Institution, 1994.

Duncan Baird Publishers, *Gods of Sun and Sacrifice – Aztec and Maya Myth*. Time-Life Books, 1997.

Earle, Sylvia A., *Sea Change*. Fawcett Columbine, 1996.

Faulkes, Anthony (translated), *Edda – Snorri Sturluson*. Everyman, 1996.

Girard, Raphael, *Esotericism of the Popul Vuh*. Theosophical University Press, 1979.

Hamblin & Christiansen, *Earth's Dynamic Systems* (seventh edition). Prentice-Hall, 1995.

Krupp, E.C., *Echoes of the Ancient Skies*. Oxford University Press, 1994.

– *Skywatchers, Shamans and Kings*. Wiley, 1997.

Levy and Salvadori, *Why the Earth Quakes*. Norton, 1997.

Levy, David, *Skywatching – the Ultimate Guide to the Universe*. HarperCollins, 1996.

Lockhart, Gary, *The Weather Companion*. Wiley, 1988.

Lovelock, James, *Gaia – The Practical Science of Planetary Medicine*. Gaia Books Ltd., 1991.

Lovelock, James, *The Ages of Gaia*. Oxford University Press, 1989.

Macdougall, J.D., *A Short History of Planet Earth*. Wiley, 1996.

Man, John, (editor), *The Encyclopaedia of Space Travel and Astronomy*. Octopus, 1979.

McPhee, John, *The Control of Nature*. Hutchison Radius, 1990.

Murck, Skinner and Porter, *Dangerous Earth an Introduction to Geologic Hazards*. Wiley, 1997.

O'Meara, John J., *The Voyage of St Brendan*. The Dolmen Press, 1985.

Pearce, Fred, *The Dammed*. The Bodley Head, 1992.

Pernetta, John, *Atlas of the Oceans*. Phillips, 1995.

Plog, Stephen, *Ancient Peoples of the American Southwest*. Thames and Hudson, 1997.

Ponting, Clive, *A Green History of the World*. Penguin 1991.

Press and Siever, *Earth* (fourth edition), Freeman, 1986.

Puku'i, Mary Kawena and Curtis, C., *Hawaiian Island Legends – Pikoi, Pele and Others*. Kamehameha Schools Press, 1996.

Reisner, Mark, *Cadillac Desert*. Penguin, 1993.

Robinson, Andrew, *Earthshock*. Thames and Hudson, 1994.

Ronan, Colin A., *The Natural History of the Universe*. BCA, 1991

Scarth, Alwyn, *Volcanoes*. UCL Press, 1994.

Selmer, Carl (editor), *Navigatio Sancti Brendani Abbatis*. Four Courts Press, 1989.

Simms, George Otto, *Brendan the Navigator*. The O'Brien Press, 1990

Skinner and Porter, *The Blue Planet*. Wiley, 1995.

Soulden, David, *Stonehenge – Mysteries of the Stones and Landscape*. English Heritage, 1997.

Tedlock, Dennis, (translated), *Popul Vuh*. Touchstone, 1985.

Titchenell, Elsa-Brita, *The Masks of Odin*. Theosophical University Press, 1988.

Van Dover, Cindy, *Deep-Ocean Journeys*. Addison-Wesley, 1996.

Whitfield, Phillip, *Our Mysterious Planet*. Cassell, 1990.

Willis, Roy (editor), *World Mythology*. Simon and Schuster, 1993.

Young, Steven B., *To the Arctic*. Wiley, 1994.

Index

The publisher and author would like to thank the following for their kind permission to reproduce the photographs in this book:

Adrian Warren 8–9, 24, 34–5, 44–5, 54–5, 57, 103, 112; **Andrew Pernick** 152–3; **Ardea London Ltd/Richard Vaughan** 23/**François Gohier** 122; **Bob Cranston** 30, 36–7, 76, 82–3, 126–7; **Clare Dornan** 169; **Corbis Bettman** 151; **Curtis Martin** 132–3, 150; **Deep Ocean Exploration and Research** 85; **Ecoscene** 154 (5); **François Gohier** 179; **Getty Images/Gerben Oppermans** 129; **Grant McDowell** 128, 163; **John Noble** 124–5, 172, 176–7; **Katherine Seward** 111, 135, 137; **Kevin Flay** 58, 79; **Kit Breen** 155; **L. Alan Cruikshank** 148; **Mariano** Advertising 162; **Mike Potts** 120–1; **NASA** 7, 10, 12–13, 14, 16, 18, 20, 25, 71, 72, 89, 96–7, 114, 116 (top), 116 (bottom), 119 (5), 142, 143, 156; **National Geophysical Data Center** 168, 170; **National Hurricane Center** 100; **Paul Watts** 136; **Planet Earth Pictures** 64–5, 86, 71, 170–1, 182; **Popperfoto** 102/**Arni Saeberg-Morgunblid** 40/**Rob Taggart** 73/ **Royal Navy** 164/**David Gray** 183; **Science Pictures Ltd** 15, 22, 24, 31, 115, 146; **Steve Nicholls** 1, 2, 28, 33, 38, 42, 43, 47, 50–1, 52, 59, 60, 62, 66, 68, 75, 78, 80, 84, 90, 91, 92, 94, 104–5, 106, 109, 130, 138–9, 140, 145, 146–7, 160, 175, 180, 184–5, 187; **US Fish and Wildlife Service** 67; **USGS** 99, 158, 166–7; **Woods Hole Oceanographic Institution** 49.